Cambridge

Elements in Global China
edited by
Ching Kwan Lee
Hong Kong University of Science and Technology,
University of California-Los Angeles

CLASH OF EMPIRES

From "Chimerica" to the "New Cold War"

Ho-fung Hung
Johns Hopkins University

CAMBRIDGE
UNIVERSITY PRESS

University Printing House, Cambridge CB2 8BS, United Kingdom

One Liberty Plaza, 20th Floor, New York, NY 10006, USA

477 Williamstown Road, Port Melbourne, VIC 3207, Australia

314–321, 3rd Floor, Plot 3, Splendor Forum, Jasola District Centre,
New Delhi – 110025, India

103 Penang Road, #05–06/07, Visioncrest Commercial, Singapore 238467

Cambridge University Press is part of the University of Cambridge.

It furthers the University's mission by disseminating knowledge in the pursuit of
education, learning, and research at the highest international levels of excellence.

www.cambridge.org
Information on this title: www.cambridge.org/9781108816212
DOI: 10.1017/9781108895897

© Ho-fung Hung 2022

First published 2022

A catalogue record for this publication is available from the British Library.

ISBN 978-1-108-81621-2 Paperback
ISSN 2632-7341 (online)
ISSN 2632-7333 (print)

Clash of Empires

From "Chimerica" to the "New Cold War"

Elements in Global China

DOI: 10.1017/9781108895897
First published online: March 2022

Ho-fung Hung
Johns Hopkins University
Author for correspondence: Ho-fung Hung, hofung@jhu.edu

Abstract: Many believe the recent deterioration in US–China relations represents a "New Cold War" rooted in ideological differences. However, such differences did not prevent the two countries from pursuing economic integration and geopolitical cooperation in the 1990s and 2000s. Ho-fung Hung argues that what underlies the change in US–China relations is the changing relationship between US–China corporations. Following China's slowdown after 2010, state-backed Chinese corporations turned increasingly aggressive when they expanded in both domestic and global markets. This was at the expense of US corporations, who then halted their previously intense lobbying for China in Washington. Simultaneously, China's export of industrial overcapacity has provoked geopolitical competition with the United States. The resulting dynamic, Hung argues, resembles interimperial rivalry among the great powers at the turn of the twentieth century.

Keywords: US–China relation, intercapitalist competition, business lobbying, Belt and Road, imperialism

ISBNs: 9781108816212 (PB), 9781108895897 (OC)
ISSNs: 2632-7341 (online), 2632-7333 (print)

Contents

1 Introduction: Political Sociology of Global Conflict

After the collapse of the Soviet Union and the end of the Cold War in the early 1990s, politicians and academics hailed the coming of a new world order in which the United States would become the lone superpower (e.g., Allison and Treverton 1992; Nye 1991). Fast forward to the 2010s, with the United States and China heading toward more confrontation over trade, technology, the South China Sea, Taiwan, and many other issues, the conception of a "New Cold War" has taken hold (Ferguson 2019; Kaplan 2019). Countries around the world are increasingly pressed to choose a side between the two giants. According to the notion of the US–China "New Cold War," the increasing tension between the two largest economies in the world has been driven by a rift in ideology and political systems: a conflict between liberal democracy and authoritarianism or a conflict between free-market capitalism and state capitalism (Macfarlane 2020; Milanovic 2019).

Some casual observers attribute the escalating tension between the United States and China to the Trump administration's recklessness. But any serious analysis points to the reality that the rivalry runs deeper than a particular administration, predating Trump and continuing into the Biden administration (see Feng 2020; Guo and He 2020; Meyers 2020). The rivalry between the two countries first became apparent in the early 2010s. In 2012, Washington launched the "Pivot to Asia" policy that increased US naval presence in the South China Sea to maintain what the United States and its allies regard as the open sea. This was in response to China's claim of sovereignty over the area and its increasingly aggressive military buildup there. The Obama administration also sped up the negotiation of the Trans-Pacific Partnership (TPP) trade agreement. This free-trade pact excluded China, with the intention of pressuring it to change its economic system, which is currently dominated by state-owned enterprises, open up its market as promised, and prevent its allegedly unfair treatment of American and other foreign companies should it seek to join. In 2014, when China launched the Asia Infrastructure Investment Bank (AIIB) as a multilateral financial institution offering loans to Asia's developing countries, the United States saw it as a direct challenge to its hegemony over development finance via the International Monetary Fund (IMF) and the World Bank. Washington chose to boycott the AIIB and called on its allies to do the same, though with little avail.

Many would explain the US–China rivalry in terms of the antagonistic differences between the two countries' political–economic models. But a major problem with this explanation is that these differences have not emerged recently. Since the Tiananmen Square Massacre of 1989 and the consolidation of Chinese Communist Party (CCP) authoritarian rule in the 1990s, it has been clear that China would not become a liberal democracy anytime soon. It was evident that the country's authoritarian regime was consolidating, not weakening, during the 1990s and the 2000s. Some have observed that Beijing's new aggressiveness in foreign affairs, revived dominance of state enterprises, and redoubled attacks on civil society started in the Hu Jintao period (2002–12) (Blumenthal 2020). Yet these ideological and political differences did not prevent the United States and China from pursuing economic integration and geopolitical cooperation in the 1990s and 2000s. The symbiosis between the two countries was very strong, leading Niall Ferguson to coin the phrase "Chimerica" to describe the singular, integrated economy formed by the union between China and America (Ferguson and Schularick 2007).

Likewise, some see the United Staes and China as having constituted a "G2" as coleaders of the world (Bergsten 2005; Zoellick and Lin 2009). Some long-standing China policy insiders in Washington, such as intelligence official and Trump China advisor Michael Pillsbury, argue US–China conflict was inevitable, as Beijing has always seen the United States as its enemy and its long-term goal since 1949 has been to topple US global leadership so as to establish its own world domination (Pillsbury 2015). True as it may be, this interpretation cannot explain why China hid its intention so well that Washington was not aware of it until the 2010s. It is noteworthy that many advocates of this view are leading voices that supported US–China symbiosis in Washington in earlier times.

We therefore need to explain why the US–China symbiosis of the 1990s and 2000s suddenly turned into rivalry in the 2010s, given that the political and economic systems of neither country underwent any fundamental, qualitative change. For this, Graham Allison's (2017) thesis of Thucycdides' trap seems to offer a clue. Drawing on the war between Sparta and Athens in ancient Greece, Allison observes a conflict between a rising power and an established power, which always jealously guards its status quo domination and seeks to hold down any new challenger, as an inevitable trajectory. Viewing the conflict between the UK and Germany and that between Russia and Japan in the early twentieth century as precedents, Allison asserts that today's US–China relationship is heading toward the same destiny of conflict. From this perspective, the United States and China remained harmonious as long as China was weak and content with being the United States' junior partner. Once China reached a certain level of capacity and confidence, however, it began to show greater ambition, and the US started to see it as a challenger. Harmony then gave way to conflict. This notion regarding the nature of US–China rivalry has inspired much writing that characterizes the relation between the two countries as edging toward "Great Power Competitions" (Colby and Mitchell 2020; Foreign Affairs 2020; Jones 2020).

Allison's explanation is neat and seems convincing. But its interpretation of US–China relations from the exclusive lens of the competition between the national states begs the question of what role the myriad international institutions, in which both countries have been active, play in ameliorating or aggravating the tension between the two. This gap has been recently filled by a new literature that complements the view on competition between great powers by bringing in the complexities of global governing institutions. These works put US–China competition in the context of the politics of global organizations, new and old, like the World Trade Organization (WTO), AIIB, and BRICS (Brazil, Russia, India, China, and South Africa) (Hopewell 2016). They translate the question concerning US–China competition into that of whether China's rise is subverting the liberal norms and international order constructed under US leadership in the aftermath of World War II (WWII), or simply continuing it with the same principle of global multilateralism (deGraaf et al. 2020).

Focusing either on competition between two individual states or how they shape and reshape norms and orders in global governing institutions, these works focus exclusively on geopolitics and stop short of addressing how the economic linkages between the United States and China contribute to their changing relations. They assume that states are autonomous actors in pursuit of power, world domination, or global governance. This assumption has been common in political science and political sociology since the "Bringing the State Back In" school reinstated the Weberian conception of state autonomy. From the Weberian perspective, an autonomous foreign policy elite's definition of national interest, and the policy orientation developed endogenously in the elite network, are the foundations for analyzing international politics. The foreign policy elite is composed of military–intelligence–diplomatic officials, think tank scholars, and elected officials with foreign policy interests (Krasner 1978; Skocpol 1985; Walt 2018). This follows Weber's assumption that state action on the international stage is driven by the "sentiment of prestige" and the pursuit of "power-position" in the world (Weber 2013 [1922]: 921–22). This perspective is a reaction to the Marxian perspective, which sees the state's foreign policy as a simple reflection of the economic imperatives of transnational corporations (Dreiling and Darves 2016; Panitch and Gindin 2013; Robinson 1996).

Beyond statist and economistic views, there have been more nuanced theories of global politics that see competition between states and transnational linkages or competition between corporate organizations as two autonomous fields that interact to shape world order and conflict (Arrighi 1994; Arrighi and Silver 1999; Van Apeldoorn and de Graaff 2016). In this Element, I draw on insights from these theories to examine the origins of US–China symbiosis in the 1990s and 2000s and its mutation into rivalry in the 2010s by connecting geopolitical relations between states and intercapitalist relations between corporations. I will focus on the meso-level interaction of corporations and states between the United States and China against the backdrop of macrostructural shifts in the global political economy.

Section 2 looks at US strategies in the 1970s to cope with its economic and hegemonic crisis by building a neoliberal global empire. The attempt succeeded and the United States had an imperial moment at the turn of the twenty-first century that witnessed a revival in US profitability and global power. Such success hinged in large part on the integration of China into the neoliberal global order. This integration was not predetermined, but made possible by a concatenation of interactions between the Chinese state and US political and economic elites. The US foreign policy elite started to define China as a geopolitical rival after the end of the Cold War, in the early 1990s. However, the emerging coalition between the CCP and US corporations turned the latter into Beijing's proxy lobbyists, restraining the US state's geopolitical impulse to pursue a hostile policy toward China.

Section 3 examines how capitalist development in China, just like capitalist development elsewhere, entered into an overaccumulation crisis aggravated by the aftermath of the 2008 global financial crisis. This overaccummulation crisis, fomenting rapid debt growth and industrial overcapacity, drove the CCP and its state-owned corporations to revive profitability by aggressively squeezing US and other foreign corporations in the Chinese market. Such confrontation pushed US corporations, which used to take the lead in ensuring an amicable US–China relationship, into stopping the restraint of the US foreign policy elite's confrontational posture toward China. In some areas, US corporations even sought the American state's assistance in intensifying competition with Chinese enterprises. Such a shift in US corporate disposition toward China underlines the rising hostility between the US and Chinese states over a whole range of issues after c. 2010.

Section 4 looks at how US–China intercapitalist competition in the Chinese market expanded into the world market when China's overaccumulation forced its corporations to expand overseas – in particular, into the developing world – at the expense of US corporate interests and geopolitical influence. This intercapitalist competition on the world stage induced the Chinese state to start carving out its sphere of influence in Asia and beyond, intensifying the geopolitical rivalry between the United States and China.

As the first and second-largest economies in the world, with combined GDP and military budgets constituting almost 40 percent and over 50 percent of the world total, respectively, the changing relationship between the United States and China is the most consequential change in world politics, determining the future of the world order, or disorder, in the twenty-first century. This Element is as much an attempt to explain changing US–China relations as it is a projection of where the global configuration of political powers is heading. In the concluding section, I explore possible scenarios of world conflict or world peace by comparing the new US–China rivalry with the interimperial rivalry among great powers in the early twentieth century.

2 Symbiosis

2.1 US-Led Neoliberal Globalization

In the aftermath of WWII, the United States led the advanced capitalist world in pursuing a high wage, high welfare, and high consumption model of growth with Keynesian regulation of the market (Arrighi 1994; Silver 2003). This paradigm of an activist government and working-class power fomented a long postwar boom in most developed economies (Brenner 2003). However, the boom ended in the late 1960s with the beginning of the stagflation crisis and corporations' falling profitability. The crisis originated partly from intensifying competition from European and Japanese manufacturers, which had fully recovered from the war, and partly from the extended period of rising wages driven by the power of organized labor (Arrighi 2007: chs. 4–6; Brenner 2003).

In an attempt to revive capitalist profitability, Washington ushered in the neoliberal revolution in the 1980s (Harvey 2007; see also Arrighi 2007: chs. 4–6; Arrighi and Silver 1999: ch. 3; Stein 2011). The crux of the neoliberal solution to the crisis in the 1980s was taming organized labor through union busting and tightening monetary policy. Free-trade policies that forced workers in advanced countries to compete with low-wage, nonunionized labor overseas was another key in supressing the power of labor to demand higher wages (Hung 2018; Hung and Thompson 2016). As such, the United States led the world into neoliberal globalization by opening its market to foreign manufactured exports in exchange for its trading partners' openness to US investment. The result has been a massive exodus of American manufacturers to low-wage countries, where consumer goods were manufactured and exported back to the United States. These dynamics have also applied to other advanced capitalist economies, fomenting the rise of the global supply chain network, the bedrock of globalization.

Since the 1980s, the United States has been running the largest trade deficit in the world, while every other major economy (China, Japan, and European countries, among others) has been running a surplus, to varying degrees, as shown in Figure 1.

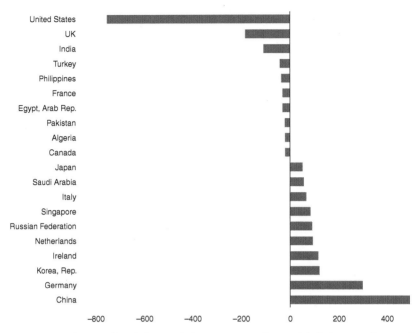

Figure 1 Balance of trade in goods in top ten surplus and deficit countries as of 2016 (in billions, current USD)
Source: World Bank a (n.d.)

In the neoliberal global economy, the United States is always "the consumer of last resort." Its huge consumer market gives it important leverage to lure other countries into the global free market (Hung 2018). The Unites States' role as the world's consumer of last resort originated from its unique political economy that historically favored consumption over investment and export. A unique feature of the US political economy is its lack of value-added tax to repress consumption and encourage saving, investment, and export – a feature in most other advanced capitalist economies (Prasad 2012). The role of the US dollar (USD) as the global reserve currency since 1945 enabled and necessitated the United States to run a massive current account deficit with the world. To maintain the dollar's grip on the world economy, the United States has to provide the world with sufficient liquidity through the outflow of its currency. This is achieved through massive US capital export and its equally massive trade deficit. Furthermore, the Unied States is the only economy in the world that can print more of its currency to cover its fiscal and current account deficit, given the global reserve currency status of the dollar (Klein and Pettis 2020: ch. 6).

Despite the expectation of the collapse of the dollar's dominance following Nixon's abolition of the dollar's gold convertibility in 1971, the USD is still the hegemonic currency in international transactions and foreign exchange reserves worldwide. The euro ranks a distant second. After its gold convertibility ended, the longevity of the dollar hegemony relied on the US global security umbrella. This enables Washington to pressure leading capitalist countries that depend on its protection to denominate their exports and foreign exchange reserves in dollars (Garvin 2003: 20; see also Eichengreen 2011: 71; Posen 2008; Strange 1980).

Many developing countries were initially resistant to neoliberal globalization. Throughout the Cold War period, the dominant paradigm of development was import substitution and state-led industrialization. Many authoritarian regimes, left and right, jealously guarded their domestic market and restricted the entry of foreign capital, leaving the economy's biggest prizes to politically well-connected and monopolistic local enterprises, which often relied on generous subsidies from the state. To draw these developing countries into US-led globalization, the United States took advantage of the international debt crisis in the 1980s. When the Federal Reserve tightened the money supply to suppress organized labor and stifle inflation in the early 1980s, the dollar's interest rate skyrocketed to over 20 percent. This sudden surge in the USD's interest rate dealt a blow to many developing and Soviet-bloc countries, which had borrowed heavily to finance their development and consumption in the 1970s. When these countries were on the verge of defaulting on their USD debt, the IMF and World Bank stepped in to offer emergency loans to keep them afloat. The loans were conditional on the debtor countries pursuing structural adjustment reforms, including privatization, capital market liberalization, and export promotion. These conditional loans became the instrument the United States used to pull many reluctant developing and Soviet-bloc countries into the global free market (Bienefeld 2000).

In sum, the US-led globalization project beginning in the 1980s was a remedy for the crisis of profitability across advanced capitalist countries. In 1993, when Clinton became the first post–Cold War American president, the United States enjoyed opportunities to expand free trade into vast new frontiers in the formerly socialist bloc and in Latin America, where the emerging North America Free Trade Agreement (NAFTA) was supposed to be the first step toward an American free-trade bloc.

At the time, China was at an economic standstill and facing political uncertainty following the Tiananmen crackdown in 1989 and the collapse of the Soviet Union in 1991. With the dissolution of the Soviet Union, the common enemy that had bound Washington and Beijing since the 1970s, Washington reevaluated its quasi-alliance with the CCP government and was not in a hurry to draw China into the orbit of globalization. Instead, the Clinton administration's foreign policy elite initially saw authoritarian China as a potential rival and prioritized human rights promotion in its China policy. The foreign policy discourse of "China threat" started to emerge in Washington, projecting China as the next major force that Washington had to confront and contain after the Soviet Union (Bernstein and Monro 1997; Callahan 2005; Huntington 1996; King 2005; Storey and Yee 2002). Surging conflicts between China and US allies in the South China Sea and the East China Sea in the mid-1990s, the Taiwan Strait Crisis in 1996, nuclear proliferation in Pakistan involving China, the United States' bombing of the Chinese embassy in Belgrade in 1999, and the US spy plane's clash with a Chinese warplane in the South China Sea in 2001 all pointed to intensifying US–China geopolitical tensions after the end of the Cold War.

As China was unscathed by the Third World debt crisis, the IMF and the World Bank had little incentive or leverage to pressure Beijing to adopt structural adjustment reforms (Hung 2016: Ch. 2–3). China's incorporation into the global free-trade order in the 1990s was neither a result of Western invitation nor of pressure. The CCP leaders themselves took the initiative to adopt market liberalization in the 1980s and to seek China's incorporation into the global free-trade system in the 1990s. Beijing even mobilized US corporations to move US–China policy from an initial human rights driven political confrontation to economic engagement. China entered the post–Cold War global free market by self-invitation.

2.2 China's Quest for the Global Free Market

In the 1980s, China's market reform was driven mostly by agricultural decollectivization and the rise of rural industries or township and village enterprises (TVEs), run by local governments. The TVEs employed surplus rural labor to manufacture consumer goods for the domestic market. Meanwhile, export-oriented industries started to grow in select southern cities that benefited from Hong Kong based manufacturing capital inflow. The export share of the economy remained small (Hung 2016: ch. 3). After the bloody crackdown of Tiananmen, market reform and the economy stalled. Following the collapse of the Soviet Union in 1991, Deng Xiaoping pushed for continuous and bolder reform to restart economic growth in his 1992 Southern Tour. Economic growth resumed, but high inflation and overheating ensued. Worse, state banks opened the flood gates, lending to local governments and state enterprises, thus fueling an investment boom that brought about growing indebtedness and trade deficit. The foreign exchange reserve fell precipitously when inflation surpassed 20 percent.

Confronted with the economic crisis, then Vice-Premier Zhu Rongji, who was in charge of economic policy at the time, moved to reign in bank lending. He tried to reorient the economy to one driven by foreign direct investment

(FDI) and exports as a remedy for the deteriorating trade deficit and shrinking foreign exchange reserve. To achieve this reorientation, he introduced a 30 percent depreciation of the Chinese RMB in January 1994 and disinvested from TVEs to release surplus rural labor for coastal export-oriented factories (Zhu 2011: 392–93).

The US market has been the largest market for East Asian export-oriented manufacturing since the 1960s. It was also the largest market for the nascent export sector in China throughout the 1980s. For Beijing's attempt to shift China's economy to export-led growth to succeed, the US market needed to remain open to Chinese manufactured exports at low tariffs. Just as the Chinese economy was at the critical juncture of moving toward export-led growth, however, US market openness to Chinese products – an openness that had been in force since the United States and China established formal diplomatic ties in 1979 – was put on hold. Immediately after Bill Clinton was inaugurated in 1993 as the first Democratic president in more than a decade, the post-Cold War foreign policy elite in the new administration, with the backing of human rights advocates who were not friendly to Beijing as well as organized labor that was not friendly to free trade, sought to link tariffs on Chinese imports to human rights improvements in China.

The particular policy that the Clinton administration sought was to link China's improvement in human rights to its Most Favored Nation (MFN) status under the international trade framework of the General Agreement on Trade and Tariffs (GATT). After WWII, international trade was regulated under GATT before it was superseded in 1995 by the World Trade Organization. Each GATT member was obliged to offer MFN status to all other GATT members, conferring exports from all members the same lowest available tariffs. During the Cold War, most Communist countries were excluded from GATT, and US trade law forbade the US government from extending MFN status to these countries. After 1974, a US president could grant MFN status to Communist countries if the country allowed its people to migrate to non-Communist countries freely. MFN status needed to be renewed annually by the White House. After each presidential renewal, Congress had sixty days to overturn the renewal, but the president could veto the overturn. A two-thirds majority of each chamber of Congress was required to override a presidential veto (Heritage Foundation 1979; Kuo 1994).

When the United States established formal diplomatic relations with Beijing in 1979, the Carter administration immediately granted China MFN status. Throughout the Reagan and George H. W. Bush eras, the White House renewed China's MFN status annually without much controversy. Before the 1990s, US–China trade was not significant, and the United States' renewal of China's MFN status was part of its geopolitical strategy to accommodate China's economic needs in exchange for cooperation in checking Soviet influence in Asia. When US–China trade took off in the late 1980s and early 1990s, organized labor in the United States, as well as textile and other labor-intensive industries in Southern States, began to voice their opposition to free trade with China. The challenge to the annual renewal in Congress of China's MFN status grew in the aftermath of the Tiananmen Square Massacre in 1989. After the bloody crackdown, anti–free trade activists, Democratic members of Congress representing organized labor, human rights advocates, and traditional anti-Communist warriors coalesced to seek an end to China's MFN status. George H. W. Bush made it clear that he would use his presidential veto power to override any Congressional attempt to stop the renewal. With Republican control of the Senate, the presidential veto should not have faced opposition, but the momentum in Congress was on the side of anti-renewal. In 1990–2, Congress attempted to add human rights conditions to China's MFN status renewal three times, declaring that China's failure to meet these human rights conditions would lead to the end of its MFN status. These human rights conditionalities twice passed both Congressional chambers, only to be vetoed by President Bush.

With the White House under the control of Republicans, who, since Nixon and Kissinger, had been committed to stable relations with China for geopolitical reasons, any Democratic opposition to the renewal of China's MFN status was futile. The situation changed, however, in 1992 when the presidential election promised a Democratic victory. During the election, free trade in general and China's MFN status became focal points of contention among the candidates. Republican George H. W. Bush, who ran for reelection, pledged to continue his administration's free trade policy, and this included the launch of NAFTA and the unconditional renewal of China's MFN status. Businessman Ross Perot ran as an independent on an anti-trade platform against NAFTA and the renewal of China's MFN status, while Democrat Bill Clinton ran on a centrist, slightly anti-trade platform. During the campaign, Clinton promised to add labor and environmental clauses to a NAFTA side agreement and also promised to stop the unconditional renewal of China's MFN status, making the renewal subject to strict human rights conditions.

Clinton's position of linking human rights to the renewal of China's MFN status can be attributed to the human rights idealists in the diplomatic establishment ever since the 1989 Tiananmen crackdown. But, more importantly, it was a response to the economic concerns of organized labor, whose support was indispensable to a Democratic victory in the presidential election. Organized labor in the United States had been concerned about rising competition from low-cost, nonunionized labor in China. So the pledge for human rights conditionality regarding China's MFN status was thinly veiled protectionist opposition to US–China trade liberalization.

In the first year of the Clinton administration, its foreign policy wing was filled with idealists predisposed to the agenda of human rights promotion. They include Secretary of State Christopher Warren, US representative to the UN Madeleine Albright, and Assistant Secretary of State for East Asian and Pacific Affairs Winston Lord (who was US ambassador to China during the 1989 Tiananmen crackdown) (Lampton 1994: 601–3, 617–18). Democratic change in Soviet-bloc countries encouraged the human rights idealists in the foreign policy establishment. Moreover, organized labor, which had been sponsoring Congressional attempts to overturn China's MFN status under the Reagan and Bush administrations, felt empowered with a new Democratic administration. Thus, Clinton announced on May 28, 1993, that the annual renewal of China's MFN status would no longer be automatic. Instead, it would be linked to the result of a presidential review of China's progress in seven areas of human rights, which covered the most contentious issues such as prison labor, the release of political prisoners, religious freedom, and the autonomy of Tibet. China's failure to improve on any two of the seven areas would lead to the termination of China's MFN status.

The end of the unconditional annual renewal of China's MFN status significantly increased American enterprises' uncertainty regarding China's business environment. China's tariff levels could go up drastically should the country lose MFN status in the coming years. Whether and how China would retaliate against American businesses already in China in the event of nonrenewal was uncertain too. Regardless of the actual result of each annual review, linking MFN status to human rights conditions effectively put the brakes on further growth of US–China trade and expansion of the US corporate supply chain into China. China's attempt to move to export-driven growth had hit a major roadblock.

2.3 Transnational Corporations, Wall Street, and Clinton's China Policy

Clinton's conditionalities invoked an aggressive lobbying effort on the part of US businesses for a delinking of human rights from trade with China. Having long relied on the veto power of a Republican president to secure the continuous renewal of MFN status, by 1993–4 businesses started to mobilize to lobby the Democrats (Destler 2005: 211–13; Lampton 1994; Sutter 1998; Zeng 2004: ch. 4). At first glance, it seems that US corporations lobbied against the human rights conditionality because they were either already operating in China and therefore hurt by this policy shift, or because they anticipated the future benefits of further liberalization of US–China trade.

An anomaly of these lobbying efforts was that, unlike many other occurrences of business lobbying where organizations like the US Chamber of Commerce and the National Association of Manufacturers led the way, in the case of China it was individual transnational corporations at the forefront of the lobbying activities (Lampton 1994; Sutter 1998; Zeng 2004: ch. 4). A further anomaly, as we shall see in the next section, was that many of the most active corporate lobbyists had no presence in China; thus, the nature of their businesses would not automatically translate into huge benefits from liberalizing US–China trade. Furthermore, some corporations that eventually gained significantly from US–China free trade, were conspicuously absent from the lobbying efforts in 1993–4. Back then, many US corporations had not yet foreseen China's centrality in globalization. In the first year of the Clinton administration, the lobbying focus for most US enterprises and business organizations was ensuring the passing of NAFTA (Hung 2020a). Keen supporters of globalization at that time saw NAFTA as the first step toward an American free-trade bloc, and few saw China, still under Communist rule, as a major new frontier of globalization.

We can gauge the relative level of involvement of different corporations in the lobbying effort for the delinking of human rights from MFN status by counting the number of times that individual corporations were mentioned in the delinking discussion in the Congressional Records for the years 1993 and 1994. Usually, an individual corporation was mentioned in connection with the MFN discussion when a petition letter signed by the corporation was included in the Record or when particular Congress members spoke on behalf of certain corporations' interests. The mention count of the corporations approximates to the varying extent of involvement of these corporations in the campaign. To verify the result, I also recorded the number of mentions of individual corporations supporting China's MFN renewal for the same period in the media, first in three major newspapers and then in all news outlets. The different counting methods coincided well. In all rankings, Boeing came out as the most active lobbyist for China's MFN renewal, closely followed by AT&T.

In terms of their actual and potential relationship to US–China trade, we could categorize all corporations into three types, as can be seen in Table 1: corporations that already had a vested interest in Chinese trade and would certainly benefit from liberalization; corporations that did not yet have many business links with China but could reasonably expect benefits from the liberalization of US–China trade in the future; and corporations whose direct

Table 1 Mentions of companies in the Congressional Record and news reports about te MFN debate, 1993–4, ranked by combined mentions in the Congressional Record and all newspapers

Rank	Company	Congressional Record	New York Times, Washington Post, Wall Street Journal	All newspapers	Combined Congressional Record and all newspapers	Business categories*
1	Boeing	115	43	317	432	3
2	AT&T	77	39	138	215	3
3	GM	101	20	53	154	2
4	McDonnell Douglas	70	15	64	134	3
5	IBM	93	5	34	127	3
6	Chrysler	67	12	49	116	2
7	GE	73	13	43	116	3
8	Nike	32	15	59	91	1
9	Sears	67	5	24	91	1
10	Ford	46	13	39	85	2
11	Motorola	40	9	38	78	3
12	Westinghouse	47	4	24	71	3
13	Coca-Cola	28	8	36	64	2
14	Hughes	27	9	36	63	3
15	Lockheed	55	2	5	60	3

Table 1 (cont.)

Rank	Company	Congressional Record	New York Times, Washington Post, Wall Street Journal	All newspapers	Combined Congressional Record and all newspapers	Business categories*
16	Exxon	56	1	3	59	3
17	Kodak	50	2	8	58	2
18	American Farm Bureau Fed.	54	0	3	57	1
19	Pepsi	37	2	15	52	2
20	Intel	43	0	6	49	2

* Business categories:

(1) Corporations that already had a vested interest in US–China trade and would undoubtedly benefit from its liberalization.

(2) Corporations that did not yet have much business with China but could reasonably expect benefits from the liberalization of US–China trade in the future.

(3) Corporations that would not directly benefit very much from the liberalization of US–China trade given the nature of their business.

Sources: ProQuest US Newsstream, www.proquest.com/usnews/advanced; Congressional Record, www.congress.gov/congressional-record.

benefits from low tariffs in respect of Chinese exports in the US market were uncertain given the nature of their business.

Many corporations that did not yet have a stake in China but could expect benefits from the liberalization of US–China trade, like Detroit's automobile companies, were quite active as China could become a big market for their exports. Those corporations that already depended on US–China trade – most notably, footwear and garment retailers that had outsourced to Chinese manufacturers early on – were not among the most active in the lobbying efforts. Most puzzling is that a group of enterprises that did not have any connection to Chinese trade and would not have obvious, direct benefits from low tariffs for Chinese exports in the US market, including telecommunication companies like AT&T, satellite companies such as Hughes Electronics, and energy corporation ExxonMobil, were among the most active in the lobbying efforts. Boeing and other aircraft makers also fall into this category because US export of aircraft to China does not go through regular trade channels and needs approval by American and Chinese authorities on an order-by-order basis. Regulation of aircraft exports by US authorities resembles regulation over the export of weapons and other sensitive technology deemed important to national security. As such, airplane sales are often linked to bilateral negotiation between the two governments. For example, the first batch of planes that Boeing sold to China was in the summer of 1972, when there was no formal trade relationship between the United States and China. The sale was a direct result of Nixon's visit to China earlier that year (Witkin 1972).

Corporations that had no direct connection with Chinese trade sent petition letters to the White House and Congressional members, having already mobilized their employees to call or write individual letters to Senators and House Representatives in their districts. Many of these companies were influential campaign donors to Congressional and presidential candidates. For example, AT&T was the biggest corporate donor among all organizational donors, contributing more than two million dollars during the 1992 election cycle (Hung 2020a: table 4). As another example, Hughes Electronics was a keen donor to Clinton's presidential campaign in 1992. In late 1993, its CEO wrote two blunt letters to Clinton, reminding him of the financial support for his campaign and requesting that the White House reconsider certain sanctions on China besides the MFN issue (Gerth 1998).

Organized labor, a key constituent of the Democratic Party, was opposed to the lobbying campaigns. Its influence contributed significantly to Clinton's pledge to link human rights conditionality to China's MFN status in the first place. Another constituent of the anti-MFN renewal coalition was Southern textile industries, which did not want to see their competitiveness eroded by low-cost Chinese imports (Zeng 2004: 112, 122). Human rights activists and Chinese dissidents in exile were also part of the coalition (Campbell 2015).

Torn between organized labor and corporate interests, in early 1994 the Clinton administration deliberated about renewing China's MFN status, even though China was nowhere near meeting the human rights conditions set in 1993. Concurrently, the rising power of the newly created National Economic Council (NEC) in the White House significantly increased Wall Street's voice in the government's decision-making process. The NEC was created through a presidential executive order on January 25, 1993 and, in 1997, Clinton referred to as "the single most significant organizational innovation that our administration has made in the White House" (cited in Krueger 2000). Robert Rubin, a veteran Wall Street banker and cochairman of Goldman Sachs, was the Council's first director. The NEC was to centralize the decision-making process related to domestic and international economic policy and oversee the implementation of the decisions made. It was modeled on the National Security Council, which was created in 1947 to centralize foreign policy decision-making at the dawn of the Cold War. Sharing many members with the powerful National Security Council, the NEC managed to seize control, from the State Department, of policies related to foreign economic relations (Dolan and Rosati 2006; Lampton 1994: 606, passim).

With Rubin as head of the NEC, the views and interests of the financial sector dominated the administration. Joseph Stiglitz, member of the Council of Economic Advisors under Clinton (1993–5) and then Chair (1995–7), pointed out that the consideration of balancing different groups' interests in the economic policymaking process was abandoned, while "[f]inance ... rule[d] supreme" and the movement of bond and stock markets became the primary policy guide (Stiglitz 2002: XIV). Likewise, David Lampton, based on his extensive interviews with Clinton-era officials, observed that "[t]he President and his economic advisors were exceptionally sensitive to movements in the financial markets .... In the first half of 1994 ... financial markets were reacting negatively to the prospect of deteriorating US–China relations" (Lampton 1994: 608).

The dominance of Wall Street's views in the White House magnified the power of corporate voices in the pro-China trade coalition at the expense of the foreign policy elite, who sought to use trade policy as a lever to undermine China's authoritarian regime. In spring 1994, the NEC, the State Department, and Democratic House of Representatives' leaders openly feuded over China's MFN status. That January, NEC Chairman Rubin had expressed his support for unconditional renewal in the *Washington Post* and suggested offering China permanent MFN status. In response, senior State Department officials protested to the White House, claiming that Rubin's comments "could weaken efforts by the Administration to maintain consistent pressure on China to improve its human rights record" (Inside US Trade 1994a). Nancy Pelosi, who chaired the US–China Working Group in the House, also criticized the proposals for unconditional renewal, emphasizing that "in the House of Representatives I think I can say unequivocally ... that the support for conditioning Most Favored Nation status for China on improvement on human rights in China and Tibet is solid" (Inside US Trade 1994b).

In the end, corporate and Wall Street power prevailed. On May 26, 1994, Clinton announced that he would renew China's MFN status without taking into consideration China's human rights progress, reversing his 1993 policy of linking human rights conditionality to the annual renewal process. Many House members tried to overturn Clinton's decision. On June 8 that year, conservative Republican congressman Gerald Solomon put forward a resolution that would revoke China's MFN status despite Clinton's decision (H. J. Res. 373, 103rd Congress). Solomon's resolution was motivated by his staunch anti-Communist stance, but it won support from some members on the left. One left-wing supporter of the resolution was Representative Bernie Sanders from Vermont, who noted that "[i]t is insane to be talking about Most Favored Nation status for a country which allows for the ruthless exploitation of its workers ... American workers cannot be, and must not be asked, to compete against the workers in China" (US Congress 1994b: 20477). The resolution was ultimately rejected by a wide margin of 75–356 in the House of Representatives.

Besides the Solomon Resolution, a group of mainstream Democrats in the House broke rank with the Clinton administration to sponsor a bill, on June 16, that put extra conditions on China's MFN status (HR 4590, 103rd Congress). The group included human rights advocates Nancy Pelosi and David Bonior, a representative of organized labor from Michigan and the former party whip of House Democrats. The bill stipulated that China's MFN benefits should only apply to private enterprises and not include any military-related or state-owned enterprises. With the backing of some of the most senior Democrats, the bill provoked an all-out mobilization of corporations in support of China's MFN renewal: 307 companies and business associations cosigned a letter to Congress opposing the bill and supporting Clinton's unconditional renewal (US Congress 1994b: 20507-09). The bill was defeated in the House by 158–270.

2.4 Beijing's Invisible Hand in Washington

The reversal of Clinton's policy on Chinese trade was a triumph of the business coalition over the coalition of organized labor, human rights advocates, the foreign policy elite motivated by human rights promotion, and labor-intensive industries in the United States. As we have seen, many of the leading corporations in the campaign, like telecommunication and oil companies, were not associated with direct benefits from US–China trade liberalization. It is also intriguing that the lobbying campaign was undertaken by individual corporations and not coordinated by business associations as is the case in many other corporate lobbying campaigns. The single most important force that brought the many corporations together into an effective coalition in favor of delinking human rights from trade with China was the Chinese state itself, which actively recruited and coordinated these corporations as its proxy lobbyists.

Clinton's decision to link human rights conditions to China's MFN status renewal came at the worst possible time for China, just as the Chinese government resolved to steer its economy to export-oriented growth in response to the economic crisis of 1992–4. Therefore, the top priority of the Chinese government was to ensure that the US market, the biggest market for its export industries, remained open at low tariffs. During the debate over delinking, Democratic Congress members noticed that lobbying firms hired by the Chinese embassy on Capitol Hill increased their activities (e.g., US Congress 1994a: 5791). But these direct lobbying efforts by the Chinese government were not effective and could have invoked a public opinion backlash (Silverstein 2007; Sutter 1998: 63).

The most important means by which Beijing tried to tilt the balance of forces in Washington in favor of delinking was its co-optation of major American corporations. As early as 1990, the economic counselor in the Chinese Embassy in the United States, Huang Wenjun, sent letters to all major US corporations, telling them to "display your impact on the US government, the Congress, as well as news mediums, do some promotion to maintain the MFN status with an aim to ... avoid the loss of bilateral interests" (cited in Weisskopf 1993). Likewise, a business writer for the *Los Angeles Times* noted that "China's leaders are pushing American companies to lobby the US government, and US business seems a bit too ready to cooperate. Some of them lectured Secretary [of State] Christopher at the US Chamber of Commerce in Beijing, criticizing his emphasis on human rights" (Flanigan 1994).

US sources provide few clues as to what Beijing offered to enlist American corporations to lobby the White House and Congress in 1993–94. A few reports show how Chinese officials explicitly used orders as a coercive means to demand that US corporations lobby Washington on China's behalf. For instance, Chinese officials once warned Boeing that Chinese state airlines would stop placing orders for its planes if it could not demonstrate its efforts to lobby for policy in Beijing's favor. The company's international strategist admitted that the company would be "toast" if it did not (Holmes 1996). Boeing is an exception regarding its frankness about pressure from China. If they did receive similar pressure, most other corporations were reluctant to admit Beijing's influence over their actions, as it could easily invite charges of collusion with an authoritarian foreign government.

Chinese state media, on the other hand, was not shy about reporting the Chinese government's efforts to enlist US companies' assistance over MFN status renewal. According to the *People's Daily*, the number of US business delegations invited to visit China peaked in 1993 and 1994 (Hung 2020a: figure 2). On many of these trips, US corporate executives signed a memorandum of understanding (MOU) with the Chinese government involving big orders and contracts. The Chinese hosts often explicitly associated these deals with their American guests' efforts in lobbying for China's MFN status renewal in 1994. Besides these US delegations to China, Chinese officials also toured the United States, visiting corporate headquarters to sign contracts or memorandum in reciprocation of their hosts' assistance over MFN. This explains the aggressiveness of lobbying by US companies that had no prior business in China and had little direct association with US–China trade. Among the corporations most active in lobbying for delinking (see Table 2), many benefited from individual incentive packages offered by the Chinese government. The deals that these corporations obtained from China in 1993–4 are summarized in Table 2.

Corporations with a vested interest in US–China trade, such as retailers that had already started outsourcing to Chinese factories, lobbied for MFN renewal out of self-interest. Here, the Chinese government does not appear to have offered any additional incentives to solicit their help. For corporations with little direct stake in US–China trade but with much influence in Washington, the Chinese government offered generous deals and Chinese officials were outspoken about these deals as rewards for the corporations' lobbying efforts.

During the Congressional debate, some members who supported delinking admitted that the discontinuation of China's MFN's status would jeopardize the lucrative contracts that China had offered individual corporations. For example, a Republican senator justified his support for delinking by giving a laundry list of corporate contracts that would be voided should China's MNF status not be renewed unconditionally. These included:

Table 2 Incentives offered by the Chinese government to selected leading US corporations for supporting the unconditional renewal of China's MFN status, 1993–4

Corporations	Incentives
AT&T	Executives visited Beijing in spring 1993 to express their support for the unconditional renewal of China's MFN status and signed MOUs pledging comprehensive long-term cooperation with China (*People's Daily*, May 23, 1993; April 29, 1994; April 30, 1994; Warwick 1994).
Boeing	China placed $4.6 billion jet order from Boeing (US Congress 1993: 12153–54).
ExxonMobil	Vice-Premier Zou Jiahua visited ExxonMobil headquarters in Texas in April 1994 to thank the company for its support for China's MFN renewal and to sign an agreement on China's offshore gas and oil field (*People's Daily*, May 4, 1994; May 7, 1994; May 28, 1994).
Hughes Aerospace	Given access to China's low-cost satellite launch; $750 million satellite and equipment contract (Gerth 1998; Gerth and Sanger 1998: Mintz 1998; Weisskopf 1993).
Farm businesses	China's agribusiness officials visited Washington in May 1993 to negotiate massive wheat purchases in ten states through the National Association of Wheat Growers (Weisskopf 1993).
GE	Chinese Vice-Premier Zou Jiahua promised GE access to energy and other sectors (*People's Daily*, December 18, 1993).
IBM	Chinese Vice-Premier Zou Jiahua visited IBM headquarters and IBM signed MOUs with China's Ministry of Commerce on technological cooperation (*People's Daily*, April 30, 1994).
McDonnell Douglas	Vice-Premier Zou Jiahua visited the McDonnell Douglas facility in California in late April 1994 to thank the company for its support for China's MFN renewal and signed a contract (*People's Daily*, May 5, 1994; May 7, 1994; Schoenberger 1994).
Various automobile companies	China made $160 million in car purchases from Detroit automakers (Weisskopf 1993).
Motorola	Chinese President Jiang Jiamin promised more access to Chinese telecommunication infrastructure (*People's Daily*, November 12, 1993).

A $120 million first-phase telecommunications plant built by Motorola; a $160 million order from the Big Three automakers; $200 million in oil-drilling equipment from companies in Louisiana, Texas, and Washington; $800 million for satellite equipment from Hughes Aerospace; a $1 billion in manufacture switches and other telecommunications equipment from AT&T; a project with ARCO Oil & Gas Co. off the southern coast of China to develop a natural gas field valued at $1.2 billion; and a projected $4.6 billion in jet orders and purchases options from Boeing Industries over the next several years (US Congress 1993: 12153–54).

AT&T is an illuminating case. The company was the most prominent among the top organizational donors to Democratic and Republican candidates in the 1992 presidential and congressional elections. Although the telecommunications company had no obvious direct stake in US–China trade, China promised it access to China's telecommunication market in 1993. In 1979, when China established formal diplomatic relations with the United States, Beijing invited AT&T to help modernize China's telecommunications network, but the company declined the offer. Throughout the 1980s, China turned to Japanese and European companies to develop its telecommunications infrastructure and, in the early 1990s, it was widely expected that China would open up its telecommunications market. Foreign telecommunications companies already in China would have had an advantage in such an opening, while AT&T would lag behind. AT&T was henceforth anxious to establish a foothold in China (Warwick 1994).

In spring 1993, AT&T executives traveled to China to express their support for the unconditional renewal of China's MFN status. During the trip, they secured a $500 million contract and signed a MOU with China's State Planning Commission. The MOU pledged ten areas of cooperation between AT&T and China, including technology transfer; joint research and development; training of Chinese nationals; and sales of equipment, network service offering, and management (Barnathan 1994; Luo 2000; Yan and Pitt 2002). AT&T China was created in mid-1993 and, in May 1994, AT&T signed an additional agreement specifying a $150 million investment in China in the following two years. The then AT&T China CEO William Warwick wrote in 1994 that "with potential business in China in the billions, AT&T is fully committed to being in China, with China, for China" (Warwick 1994: 274).

AT&T thus led the the lobbying efforts for China's MFN unconditional renewal. But after the 1994 delinking decision, matters deteriorated for AT&T in China. It had been pushed aside by China's state-owned telecommunication giants, which received heavy regulatory and financial support from the Chinese government. Its fortunes in China fell far short of its original expectations as outlined in its 1993–4 MOUs with Beijing. Today, the company's presence in the Chinese telecommunication market is minimal (Johnson 2000; Lau 2006; Walter and Howie 2012: 156–64). I will return to this case in the next section.

Some of the biggest eventual winners from trade liberalization with China were conspicuously absent in the lobbying efforts during 1993–4. Apple Inc. and Walmart are two examples. Apple was already ranked sixty-seventh in the 1994 Fortune 500 list, and was on the rise to become a nationwide retail giant. However, it was nowhere to be found in the corporate lobbying campaign for China's MFN renewal. Apple was not even among the 307 signatories of the corporate letter supporting delinking during the final showdown of Congress's debate in August 1994. And it was not among the corporations courted by Beijing.

In the early 1990s, such corporations were reluctant to move production to China. As the leading computer maker at the time, Apple was aggressively expanding its manufacturing facilities in California and Colorado. It was not until 1997–8, when the company hired Steve Jobs as president and Tim Cook as vice president of Worldwide Operation after it suffered a serious setback because of unsatisfactory product launches, that it started to move its assembly lines to China as a cost-cutting and profit-reviving strategy (Duhigg and Bradsher 2012; LEM 2006; Prince and Plank 2012; Weinberger 2017). Apple was not, therefore, active in pushing for US–China trade liberalization in 1993–4. It was opportunistic in that it benefited from liberalization during its profitability crisis only after liberalization had become a reality. Similar examples can be found among some of Walmart's main textile suppliers such as Derby Hosiery, based in Kentucky, which refrained from moving to China during the 1990s and relocated there only after US–China free trade had advanced in full force in the early 2000s (Sebenius and Knebel 2010; Smith 2012: 251–52).

In sum, in the first year of the Clinton administration, Washington's foreign policy elite prioritized trade as a lever to promote human rights in China. The Communist party–state in China managed to sway US policy by mobilizing some of the most powerful US corporations to become its "proxy lobbyists" and force the Democratic government to put free trade with China ahead of political liberalization (Wagreich 2013). As an ex post justification, the Clinton administration fomented a theory of "constructive engagement," according to which free trade with China could empower China's private enterprises and the middle class, which would in turn push for political liberalization. In any event, Beijing successfully invited itself into the US-led global free trade order without compromising on its authoritarian one-party rule.

The delinking of China's MFN status from human rights consideration was a critical turning point in US–China trade liberalization. Both the United

States' embrace of global free trade – as the biggest consumer in the world – and China's integration into the global trading system – as its largest exporter – have grown continuously since the mid-1990s. Clinton's reversal of policy by unconditionally approving China's MFN status paved the way for the administration to grant Permanent Normal Trade Relation (PNTR) status to China in 2000 ("Most Favored Nation" was renamed "Normal Trade Relation" in 1998); this cleared the last major hurdle to China's accession to the WTO in 2001. By the time the US–China PNTR debate reached Congress in 2000, years of US–China trade liberalization had created a self-sustaining vested interest in Chinese trade in the corporate sector that could spontaneously lobby for further liberalization (Dreiling and Darves 2016: 223–27; Skonieczny 2018). The resulting US–China economic symbiosis, as well as US corporate interests, became significant restrainers of the persistent tendency in Washington's diplomatic–military establishment that projects Beijing as a major geopolitical rival.

China's WTO accession contributed to the peaking of the China boom and US financial prosperity in the 2000s. With its low-wage regime and skewed income distribution, China consistently manufactured more than it consumed and relied heavily on the global market to absorb its productive capacity. The United States constituted the single most important market for China's exports, and has only recently been surpassed by the European Union. China's export-oriented industries' rapid expansion has made China the biggest exporter, of all Asian exporters, to the United States (Hung 2016: table 3.6).

Besides the export sector, China's fixed-asset investment, including infrastructure and housing construction undertaken mostly by the state sector, has been another engine of the China boom. But most of the fixed-asset investment in the Chinese economy has been financed by bank lending. A large portion of the banking system's liquidity originates from a "sterilization" process in which exporters surrender their foreign exchange earnings to state banks in exchange for equivalent RMB issued by the People's Bank of China, China's central bank. In other words, the expanding credit that fueled China's investment originates largely from China's trade surplus and the export sector. Therefore, the supposed twin-engine of investment and export in China's economic boom is, after all, a single-engine of export (Hung 2016: ch. 3).

The overwhelming majority of China's exports across the world has been invoiced in USD and the chronic trade surplus enabled China's central bank to rake in an increasing amount of USD to build up its foreign exchange reserve. Following in the footstep of Japan and the four Asian Tigers (South

Korea, Taiwan, Hong Kong, and Singapore), but on a much larger scale, China invested its foreign reserves in US Treasury bonds, the safest and most liquid USD-denominated assets. This investment helped finance the United States' expanding fiscal deficit. China's holding of US Treasury bonds has increased with the growth of its foreign reserves since 2001. It became the world's largest foreign holder of US Treasuries in 2008 and, in in the decade after the 2008 financial crisis, China's holding of US Treasuries doubled (Hung 2016: ch. 5).

The US consumer market and Washington's policy of integrating China into the global free trade system enabled the latter's export-driven economic ascendancy. China's low-cost exports fueled a consumption boom in the United States, while China's recycling of its USD earnings in US government bonds helped finance America's expanding fiscal deficit. It also kept the US interest rate low, fueling the financialization and finance-led prosperity of the US economy. Naill Ferguson has characterized this economic symbiosis, which Beijing sought and successfully secured at a critical juncture in 1993–4, as a "Chimerica" formation, as if the two countries had integrated into a single economy (Ferguson and Schularick 2007).

By the end of the Clinton administration, it had become clear that the post–Cold War global order was plagued by frequent regional geopolitical crises in the vacuum created by the Soviet collapse (e.g., the Kosovo War), and by financial crises in the unregulated global free market (from the Mexicon peso crisis of 1994 to the Asian financial crisis of 1997–8). The former required increased US military intervention in geopolitical hotspots, and the latter necessitated US-led financial intervention to bail out afflicted economies and banks. Both generated an ever-increasing fiscal burden on the American state.

US foreign military interventions grew in the 2000s with the wars in Iraq and Afghanistan. Its bailout operations amid increasingly serious and widespread financial crises, culminating in the global financial crisis of 2008, also grew. These interventions pushed the United States further along the path of a costly global empire (Hardt and Negri 2000; Harvey 2005; Ikenberry 2004; Panitch and Gindin 2013). China's low-cost manufactured exports and investment in US government debt under the Chimerica formation became an ever more important economic and fiscal foundation of US empire-making. In the 2000s, China also assisted the United States in containing geopolitical risks in Asia, such as the North Korean nuclear crisis, when America was preoccupied in Central Asia and the Middle East. In the heyday of Chimerica, China became an indispensable helper to the US global empire.

3 Intercapitalist Competition

3.1 Party–State Capitalism vs US Corporations

China's free-market reform of the 1990s turned the country into a capitalist economy – in the sense that the imperative of capital accumulation now drives most economic activities; however, China's economic system has not converged with the free-market capitalism that the United States envisioned. Three decades after China's incorporation into the global market, the state maintains control over the economy in the form of state-owned enterprises (SOEs). Private property rights have not been fully established, leaving the state as the ultimate owner of all land property, with private capitalists having no more than temporary rights to the use of land (Hung 2020b).

China's export boom facilitated the rise of the private sector in China, as small and medium private enterprises, both local and foreign, dominated China's export sector. However, Beijing did not relinquish dominance of state-owned companies in key sectors, including finance, telecommunications, energy, steel, automobile, among others. While many state-owned giants were restructured in the image of US corporations, shedding nearly all of their social functions such as providing housing and healthcare to employees, many of the largest companies were still controlled by local or central government through direct state ownership or "politically motivated state shareholding" of public companies (Wang 2015). Chinese companies in the Global Fortune 500 list grew from 10 in 2000 to 124 in 2020. Of those 124 companies, 91 are SOEs (Kennedy 2020). The dominance of state companies in key sectors is shown in Table 3.

It is noteworthy that many large, nominally private companies, like Huawei and Alibaba, remained closely linked to the CCP via party committees in the companies and the companies' connection with powerful factions within the CCP. China's state capitalism departs from state capitalism in other countries in that the power of the CCP in the economy goes far beyond SOEs. Some, therefore, conceptualize China's political economy as a unique "party-state capitalism" (Pearson et al. 2020).

The continuous dominance of the state sector was, to a large extent, founded on the thriving export sector, which has been the source of the Chinese economy's dynamism and profitability. Export enterprises, either foreign (like Taiwanese Foxconn as a subcontractor of US high-tech firms) or domestic (such as Huawei and Xiaomi that exported their telecommunication devices overseas) received various export subsidies such as export credits and tax rebates from the state that boosted their vibrancy (Defever and Riaño 2013; Marino 2018). China's central bank had long pegged the RMB to the USD,

Table 3 Total industrial assets owned by state-owned/state-holding enterprises, private enterprises, and foreign enterprises: national total and major sectors as of 2018

Sector	Total (100 billion Yuan)	State enterprises (100 billion yuan)	Private enterprises (100 billion yuan)	Foreign enterprises (100 billon yuan)
National total	1134.4	439.9	239.3	224.4
Mining and washing coal	55.1	41.8	4.8	1.4
Extraction of petroleum and natural gas	19.3	18.5	0.02	0.8
Mining and processing of ferrous metal ores	9.9	6.6	1.9	0.2
Processing of food from agricultural products	30.8	1.9	12.1	6.0
Manufacture of tobacco	10.9	10.8	0.03	0.02
Manufacture of textiles	21.8	1.2	10.0	4.2
Processing of petroleum, coal, and other fuels	31.5	15.3	6.7	3.1
Manufacture of raw chemical materials and chemical products	74.9	21.9	17.9	15.9
Manufacture of nonmetallic mineral products	48.5	9.0	18.7	5.9
Smelting and pressing of ferrous metals	61.1	32.3	13.0	5.7
Smelting and pressing of nonferrous metals	40.3	15.5	7.6	5.3
Manufacture of automobiles	79.2	36.6	11.3	30.4
Manufacture of railway, ship, aerospace, and other transport equipment	16.4	7.5	3.6	3.3
Manufacture of electrical machinery and apparatus	69.0	9.2	19.1	14.0
Manufacture of computers, communication equipment, and other electronic equipment	101.6	17.5	15.0	46.5
Production and supply of electric power and heat power	147.5	128.1	5.6	7.7

Source: National Bureau of Statistics of China (n.d.).

preventing it from appreciating as fast as export growth for a prolonged period of time. Whether this constitutes a form of potent subsidies to the export sector is a topic of heated debate that I will turn to in Section 3.3.

The foreign exchange reserves the export sector generated have provided the foundation for the expansion of state bank credit, most of which went to well-connected state enterprises or financial vehicles to support their profitless investment and growth (Rutkowski 2015). Figures 2 and 3 compare the indebtedness and profitability between state and private companies. They show that state companies have been far more indebted while being much less profitable.

Different state sectors became the fiefdoms of different elite factions within the CCP (Foster 2010; Lombardi and Malkin 2017). The division of the state sector between elite families created a balance of power, stabilizing the "collective leadership" of the party–state during the China boom in the 1990s and 2000s.

When China's export-led boom faltered during the global financial crisis in 2008, the Chinese government responded by unleashing an aggressive stimulus program that successfully fostered a strong economic recovery driven by debt-financed fixed-asset investment. The weakening of the export engine and the reckless investment expansion of the state sector financed by state banks during the 2009–10 recovery created a mammoth debt bubble that was no longer matched by the growth in the foreign exchange reserve. Between 2008 and late 2017, outstanding debt in China soared from 148 percent of GDP to over 250 percent. The surge of loans during the 2020 COVID-19 pandemic pushed the share to more than 330 percent (Institute of International Finance 2020).

The redundant capacity and infrastructure resulting from the debt-fueled economic rebound have not been profitable. Figure 2 shows that the state sector's indebtedness surged after the stimulus, while Figure 3 shows profit-to-asset ratio fell continuously across both private and state sectors after c. 2010. Economic slowdown and surge of liquidity in the form of local currency debt without commensurate expansion of foreign exchange reserves generated pressure for capital flight. It resulted in a stock market meltdown and sharp devaluation of the RMB in 2015–16; the economy only stabilized in 2016 because of tightening capital controls (Merics 2019). The banking system often injected rounds of new loans into the economy to prevent it from further slowing. These recurrent and ever-larger loan surges further increased indebtedness. The impasse in the Chinese economy is illustrated by the stagnation of its manufacturing expansion, as shown in the manufacturing Purchasing Manager Index (PMI), a lead indicator of manufacturing activities (Figure 4). Ever since the 2009–10 recovery fizzled out, the PMI has hovered around the stagnation line of fifty. Comparing the new

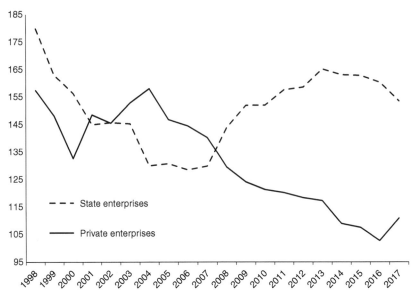

Figure 2 Liability to equity ratio in state and private enterprises (%)
Source: National Bureau of Statistics of China (n.d.).

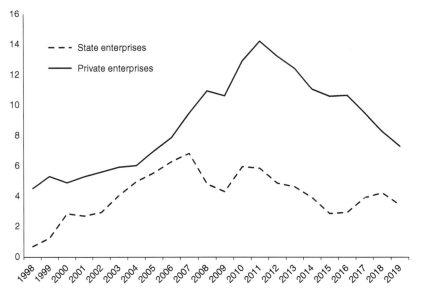

Figure 3 Profit-to-asset ratio in state and private enterprises (%)
Source: National Bureau of Statistics of China (n.d.).

loan data with the PMI, we can see the diminishing effectiveness of loan stimulus: it took ever-larger loans to generate the economy's ever- smaller rebound after the 2009–10 crisis. China's political economy has developed a debt addiction.

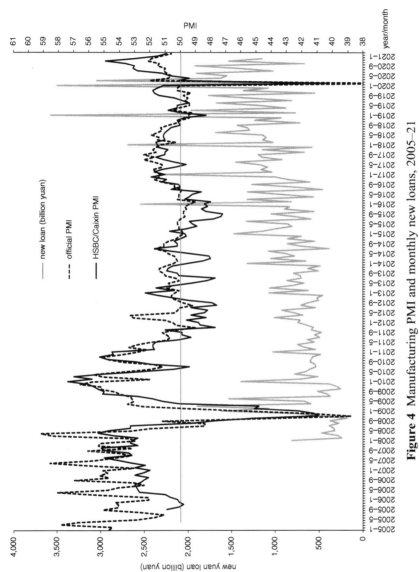

Figure 4 Manufacturing PMI and monthly new loans, 2005–21

Source: National Bureau Statistics of China (various dates), Purchasing Managers Index Press Release (e.g., October 2021, https://bit.ly/3FBCi5j); Caixin (n.d.) (various dates).

Growth slowdown and worsening indebtedness motivated the party–state elite to accelerate their squeeze on the private sector and foreign companies, as well as intensifying interparty–state elite conflict when the end of high-speed growth threatened the legitimacy of the party–state. Against this backdrop, Xi Jinping, who became the party–state's supreme leader in 2012, launched a series of initiatives to concentrate decision-making power, moving from the party–state's mode of "collective leadership" governance to autocratic rule (Choi et al 2021; Shirk 2018). This has accelerated a longer-term institutional centralization of CCP rule since the early 2000s (Fewsmith and Nathan 2019; Liu et al. 2018). The centralization process culminated in Xi's successful bid to abolish the two five-year terms limit for state president embedded in the 1982 Constitution, effectively making him a life-long dictator in March 2018. The statist turn of the Chinese economy, which started under Hu Jintao before the global financial crisis of 2008, redoubled during the post-crisis slowdown under Xi Jinping (Blumenthal 2020; Lardy 2019).

The acceleration of China's statist turn under Xi further hardened the US foreign policy elite's view of China (Campbell and Ratner 2018). Beijing's assessment of US terminal decline in the aftermath of the 2008 global financial crisis emboldened it to adopt a more confrontational stance across a range of geopolitical issues (Blanchette 2021). In the 2010s, when the United States started to exonerate itself from the wars in the Middle East, Washington turned its attention to countenancing China as a geopolitical rival under Obama's "Pivot to Asia" policy. More importantly, the accelerating statist turn of the Chinese economy was at the expense of US corporations' interests in China. This shift is much more significant in turning US–China policy toward a more confrontational mode.

In the last section, we saw how Beijing promised access to China's vast market to lure US corporations to become proxy lobbyists and influence US–China policy in its favor. These corporations became keen advocates of Clinton's engagement policy that put human rights issues second to pursuing unconditional free trade with China. US corporations also became a key deterrent to the escalation of particular geopolitical incidents and facilitated quick, reconciliatory resolutions to crises such as the Taiwan missile crisis in 1996, the US bombing of the Chinese embassy in Belgrade in 1999, and the clash between a US spy plane and a Chinese fighter jet over the South China Sea in 2001. Notable corporate CEOs often played the role of messengers between US and Chinese leaders, becoming unofficial diplomats between the two countries (see, e.g., Kranish 2018). Powerful American corporations were the glue, stabilizer, and fuel for the Chimerica formation.

For many of these corporations – most notably Apple, Walmart, and GM – such efforts paid off, as the expansion of their revenues in China became a key driver of growth. But not all corporations were happy about the China market after making extraordinary efforts to ensure China's low-tariff access to the US market in the early 1990s. For example, AT&T was the leading corporation in the campaign to delink China's MFN status from human rights conditions in 1993–4, as we saw in the last section. At the time, AT&T was enthused by the MOUs it signed with the Chinese government, expecting that Beijing would open up its telecommunications market in return. After the delinking was achieved, and despite its initial signal that it would open up the telecommunications market, Beijing became adamant in protecting domestic state giants like China Telecom. It tightened regulation in 1998 to ban foreign telecommunications companies from using legal loopholes to buy stakes in local providers (Johnson 2000). By 2000, AT&T's business as a service provider in China was restricted to a 25 percent stake in a joint venture whose operations were confined to Shanghai (Bolande 2001). Its minimal presence in China was far from what it had expected in 1993–4.

AT&T was not alone. Hughes Aerospace, which was also pivotal in lobbying the Clinton administration on delinking in 1993–4, initially benefited from the Chinese government's offer to launch its commercial satellite into earth's orbit at half the price of European or US rockets (Mintz 1998). In 1995, a Chinese rocket exploded during launch, destroying Hughes' satellite. The Chinese launcher refused compensatation and requested that Hughes hand over technical data that could improve the reliability of a future launch. Hughes complied and shared the data. However, the transfer of the relevant technology and data was sanctioned by the US government on national security grounds. The technologies and data would benefit China's ballistic missile program, which allegedly would boost China's assistance to the missile programs in Pakistan and Iran. The US government subsequently launched an investigation into Hughes and other US companies that were involved. In 2003, Hughes and the other companies paid $32 million to the US government in a settlement (Gerth and Sanger 1998; Mintz 1998; Pae 2003; Washington Post 1998).

In the 1990s and 2000s, cases of US corporations' troubled China adventures were exceptions rather than the rule. Most corporations rushing to establish themselves in China saw tremendous gains. But the challenges that AT&T and Hughes confronted – restrictive market access in contrast to what was promised and the pressure to transfer sensitive technology – were precursors of what many other US corporations were to face in China. After the global financial crisis rebound of 2009–10, there were increasing reports of US corporations being squeezed by their Chinese competitors, which were often aided by government regulators and subsidized by low-cost loans from state banks. Complaints mounted that the Chinese government pressured US corporations, subtly or explicitly, to transfer their technology to their Chinese joint-venture partners, who then became their competitors by selling similar services or products at much lower prices (Blustein 2019; Wei and Davis 2018). The anti-monopoly law implemented in 2008 and the cybersecurity law passed in 2016 were increasingly and disproportionally used against foreign companies, jeopardizing US corporations' market access, intellectual property rights, and sensitive customer data in China (Maranto 2020; Yang and Burkitt 2014).

The American Chamber of Commerce in China conducts an annual survey among its members to gauge the business climate for US enterprises. Since 2010, a growing number of American businesses have found China increasingly unwelcome; in 2018 only 20 percent said they felt "more welcome than before." Among the challenges American businesses say they are facing in China, Chinese authorities' unfair treatment has been cited as a persistent problem. The most frequently mentioned areas in which US corporations feel unfairly treated in comparison to their Chinese competitors are market access and enforcement of government regulations (Amcham China 2018, 2019). In the 2018 survey, half of the US companies in China expressed concerns that inadequate intellectual property protection limited their investment in China, in comparison with 20–30 percent that indicated that such concerns had no effect at all (Amcham China 2019: 62).

Amid a deteriorating business environment, US companies choosing not to expand, or to expand by less than 10 percent over the last year, rose from 58 percent in 2009 to 73 percent in 2019. In contrast, the percentage of US companies that expanded by more than 20 percent over the last year fell from 33 percent to 13 percent over the same period. US corporations that had relocated or considered relocating capacity outside China jumped from 11 percent in 2013, when the question was first asked in the survey, to 25 percent in 2016, and has stayed at around 20 percent since (Amcham China various years).

The US–China Business Council, a lobbying group that played a significant role in bringing fast and deep US–China economic integration in the 1990s, published a report in 2017 based on a survey of its member companies that showed the same grievances about China. Of the companies surveyed. 48 percent expressed less optimism about the business climate than three years previously, and 57 percent complained the Chinese authorities did not live up to their promise of reform and improvement of the business environment. The companies complained about the Chinese government's bias toward domestic companies (91 percent) and voiced concerns about intellectual property

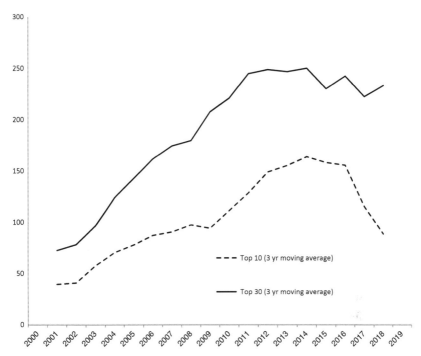

Figure 5 Mention of China in annual report of the top ten and top thirty US
Fortune 500 companies, 2000–19
Source: SEC 10-K filings of various companies.

protection in China (94 percent); 19 percent said they had been directly asked to
transfer technology to Chinese companies (Inside US Trade 2017).

The dampened enthusiasm of US corporations for China is reflected in the
general fall in China exposure among the biggest corporations in the United
States. I constructed a database that uses the number of mentions of "China" in
the annual 10-K report that the top ten Fortune 500 companies filed to the US
Securities and Exchange Commission (SEC) to indicate these companies'
exposure in China either through sales or investment.

As shown in Figure 5, the top ten companies' exposure to China dropped
precipitously from about 2014, following rapid growth in earlier periods. For
example, GMs' mention of China in its report stayed in single digits from 2000–
4. It grew to the teens in 2005 and then increased steadily to 60–70 mentions in
2014, where it stayed. There is also an apparent rise in companies in the top ten
with little China exposure, replacing those with significant China exposure.
Examples include providers of healthcare and health insurance like
UnitedHealth Group and CVS Health. These two trends have combined to
generate a fall in China exposure among the top ten companies. If we expand

the list to the top thirty companies, we see that American companies' exposure to China stopped growing after around 2010. All this suggests that while China has been at the frontier of profit when the United States' largest corporations expanded rapidly in the first decade after China's accession to the WTO, this expansion simply ceased or even reversed after 2010.

3.2 US Corporate Lawsuits against Chinese Entities

While the increasing pressure that US corporations faced in the Chinese market led to the dampening of corporate expansion in China in general, some US corporations caught up in a dispute with their Chinese partners and competitors, or allegedly receiving biased treatment from the Chinese authorities, increasingly resort to legal action in an attempt to redress the problem. Conflict over the loss of US companies' intellectual property to their Chinese partners, competitors, or the Chinese state has been the main source of US corporate lawsuits against Chinese entities.

A central goal of Beijing's statist economic policy was to leapfrog China's technological upgrading at the expense of the United States. This ambition was fully revealed in the "Made in China 2025" initiative in 2015 (Zenglein and Holzmann 2019). Although the number of patents registered in China has risen rapidly over the last decade (WIPO 2020), more nuanced analysis shows that many of those patents were worthless from a commercial standpoint. In fact, more than 90 percent of China-registered patents were not renewed after five years (Chen 2018; see also Hu et al. 2017). This lack of commercially viable innovation, despite vast government resources for this purpose and the sheer number of patents, illustrates the limit of China's progress in indigenous innovation, particularly in the dominant state sector dubbed the "paper tigers" of innovation (Fuller 2016: chs. 3 and 4). The lack of protection of intellectual property rights stands in the way of local innovation (Appelbaum et al. 2018). The inadequate progress in China's state-led innovation manifests in China's lack of technological self-sufficiency. When Chinese manufactured products move up the technological ladder, China's dependence on foreign technology increases. The intellectual property balance of payment in Figure 6 shows that China is still largely an intellectual property deficit country, meaning it pays a lot more for foreign patents and copyrights than foreign entities pay for Chinese ones. Moreover, this deficit has been expanding.

Given the limits of its homegrown innovation system, the party–state's drive to attain technological self-sufficiency hinges on controversial and at times illegal appropriation of technology from foreign companies, including outright economic espionage. The result is a rising number of lawsuit initiated by US corporations against Chinese entities over intellectual property rights. These often involve some

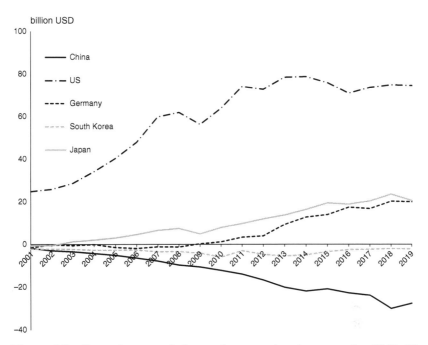

Figure 6 Intellectual property balance of payment in select countries, 2001–19
Source: World Bank a (n.d.).

of the most prominent US companies. For example, Dupont Chemicals was one of the pioneers that, in 2004, started a joint venture with a Chinese company to use its new technology to turn corn into textile materials (Forbes 2005). In 2006, it licensed the technology to Zhangjiagang Glory Chemical Industry Company in China; but from about 2013 it suspected its Chinese partners were using its technology to produce the same products at much lower prices. When Dupont started to take legal action against its Chinese partners, it received a warning from the Chinese authorities, pressuring it to drop the case. In December 2017, Chinese anti-monopoly investigators appeared in Dupont Shanghai offices, "demanding passwords to the company's worldwide research networks … [i]nvestigators printed documents, seized computers, and intimidated employees, even accompanying some when they went to the bathroom" (Davis and Wei 2020a: 250). Fearing for its business prospects in China, Dupont eventually withdrew its case.

Motorola, another leading company that moved to China as early as the mid-1990s, had a similar experience. In 2010, Motorola sued Huawei Technologies for stealing its wireless network technology. The Chinese Ministry of Commerce put pressure on Motorola by initiating an anti-monopoly investigation. Ultimately, Motorola dropped the lawsuit and, in 2011, it sold its wireless business to China's Lenovo Group (Davis and Wei 2020a: 121).

As the Chinese courts have been controlled by the party–state and US companies may have considered the courts to be biased toward the Chinese defendants, many of these lawsuits were filed in US courts against Chinese entities that have businesses in the United States. For example, American Superconductor (AMSC), a Massachusetts high-tech firm that manufactured essential high-tech components and software drivers for wind turbines, was a rising star in green technology and openly praised by President Obama. Its business expanded rapidly when one of its customers, Sinovel, a Chinese state-owned wind turbine company connected to the family of Wen Jiabao (Premier of China 2003–13), began to receive generous state support to ramp up its wind turbine production for Chinese as well as international markets. Sinovel's order constituted three-quarters of AMSC's business. However, in 2011 Sinovel suddenly refused to accept and pay for a shipment from AMSC without giving a clear reason. Losing its biggest customer, AMSC's stock price plummeted and the company nearly went bankrupt. After a lengthy investigation, AMSC found out that Sinovel had bribed an employee in AMSC's European office to download its product source codes. The Austrian court found the employee guilty and imprisoned him. AMSC then sued Sinovel, seeking compensation for its economic loss in a US court. In 2018, the court found Sinovel guilty of theft of trade secrets and ordered it to pay more than $59 million in compensation.

In a media interview, the AMSC CEO expressed indignation that the legal victory was not enough to make up for the loss that AMSC suffered (Department of Justice 2018; Zarroli 2018). The AMSC CEO, having severed all its business ties with China, spoke frankly about the risk that all US businesses face in China:

> The rules are set up in a way that the local brands will win . . . . Participation in the Chinese market is for Chinese companies only. Your participation as a Western company, at least to date, is a mirage. They're there to bring you in, be able to figure a way to harvest whatever they can from you, and then spit you out when you're no longer useful (cited in Zarroli 2018).

Not all US companies' litigation against Chinese companies in US courts end well like it did for AMSC. Most of the US companies involved have operations in China, and the Chinese companies litigated against could countersue in a Chinese court as revenge. One such case is Veeco Instruments Inc., which produced advanced machinery for the production of LED chips and supplied the booming chip industry in China. Around 2012, Veeco found out that its main Chinese competitors, AMEC of Shanghai, obtained its technology and produced a much cheaper version of its products. Veeco sued AMEC in a US court. In 2017, the court found in favor of Veeco and blocked AMEC from purchasing critical

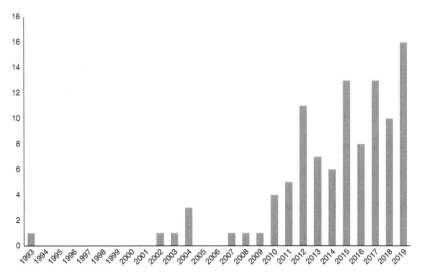

Figure 7 Count of US corporate lawsuits against Chinese entities on
intellectual property issues in US Courts, 1993–2019
Source: LexisNexis (n.d.).

components from the United States for making the machines. In response, AMEC
filed a lawsuit against Veeco for patent infringement in a Chinese court in Fujian,
where Veeco maintained a production facility. The Chinese court agreed with
AMEC and did not even notify Veeco of the hearing. Just one month after the US
court ruled in Veeco's favor, the Fujian court ruled in favor of AMEC and blocked
Veeco from selling its machines in China. Being shut out from the Chinese market
would spell financial disaster for Veeco, and it finally resorted to a private
settlement with AMEC outside the court (Davis and Wei 2020a: 262).

The lawsuits by AMSC and Veeco are by no means isolated cases. Figure 7
shows that the aggregate number of lawsuits filed by US companies against
Chinese entities related to intellectual property right in US courts rose steadily
in the early 2000s, then jumped after 2009 in the aftermath of the global
financial crisis and subsequent Chinese stimulus.

The majority of these cases follows a typical pattern. They involve US
companies, with or without businesses in China, whose employees are bribed
or manipulated to appropriate essential trade secrets and hand them over to
Chinese competitors, who then sell similar products at much lower prices and
take the original company's market share in China and elsewhere in the world.
The relation between the employee who appropriates the trade secret and the
Chinese competitor that obtains the technology varies from case to case. In
some cases, the employee, after obtaining the trade secret, reaches out to the

Chinese competitor of the victim company to offer the trade secret for a price.[1] In other cases, the employees form new companies in China to produce the same products and purposely approach the customers of the victim companies to offer cheaper alternative products.[2] There are cases in which the employees appropriating the trade secret were spies deliberately sent from Chinese companies or even the Chinese government to target particular technologies owned by certain companies. In one case, the US company's employee responsible for the trade secret appropriation had been recruited by high-level officials of the Chinese State Council to target a specific key technology owned by Dupont. The employee acted under "directives" from Beijing for more than a decade. In the end, the FBI became involved in the case, and in 2014 the indicted employee was sentenced to fifteen years imprisonment for economic espionage.[3]

Not all victims of intellectual property appropriation choose legal action. There are cases in which US companies, aware of the size of the Chinese market and thus wanting to avoid animosity with the Chinese authorities, choose to adapt rather than fight the infringement of their intellectual property rights. For example, Vermeer, a manufacturer of heavy agricultural and industrial equipment, has been exporting motorized drilling machines and other heavy machinery to China since the 1990s. In the 2000s, it found that XCMG, a local state company in Xuzhou, was selling copycat machines at much lower prices. Vermeer did not take any action but learned to innovate fast enough to stay ahead of the Chinese copycat. It also adapted by no longer selling the most advanced machine in the Chinese market. Instead, it sold more simplified, lower-cost versions of its machines in China. XCMG, as well as other heavy machinery manufacturers in China such as Sany and Zoomlion, has reportedly been thriving on selling products that are strikingly similar to designs by Vermeer and other leading construction and mining machine makers, like Caterpillar and Liebherr (Hook 2013; Mining 2020). Many of these manufacturers have not taken legal action, seemingly for the sake of the continuous goodwill they rely on in China.

---

[1] For example, Magnesita Refractories Co. v. Tianjin New Century Refratories Co., 2019 US Dist. LEXIS 32559. https://advance.lexis.com/api/document?id=urn:contentItem:5VJ2-TKW1-F8D9-M2SF-00000-00&idtype=PID&context=1516831.

[2] For example, Austar Int'l. Ltd. v. Austarpharma LLC, 425 F. Supp. 3d 336. https://advance.lexis.com/api/document?collection=cases&id=urn:contentItem:5XKW-X0T1-F361-M50S-00000-00&context=.

[3] For example, United States v. Liew. 856 F. 3d 585. https://advance.lexis.com/api/document?id=urn:contentItem:5NG8-61S1-F04K-V05B-00000-00&idtype=PID&context=1516831.
"Walter Liew Sentenced to Fifteen Years in Prison for Economic Espionage." US Department of Justice. July 11, 2014. www.justice.gov/usao-ndca/pr/walter-liew-sentenced-fifteen-years-prison-economic-espionage.

Some US corporations have tried to deal with the intensifying and allegedly unfair competition from Chinese companies by acquiring Chinese competitors. However, the Chinese authorities often step in to forestall such attempts. The party–state's goal is to cultivate state-owned champions to outcompete foreign companies and not to let them fall into foreign companies' hands. For example, in 2005 Carlyle Group in the United States attempted to acquire XCMG and Beijing became aware of this attempt. In an effort to prevent foreign companies from monopolizing the construction machine manufacturing business, the Chinese government intervened to find a buyer to outcompete Carlyle's offer. Eventually, XCMG became a central government controlled state enterprise (Davis and Wei 2020a: 411–13).

The party–state's shortcut to technological upgrading not only brings about economic espionage on the part of individuals, but also governmental coercion of foreign companies. Since 2010, allegations that the Chinese government has forced US companies in China to hand over their trade secrets to Chinese competitors as a precondition for continuous market access have soared (Inside US Trade 2012). This open governmental pressure has forced US corporations to go beyond individualized legal means and coalesce into corporate collective action to influence the US state, urging it to press Beijing for systemic improvements in the business environment.

3.3 From Beijing's "Proxy Lobbyists" to "Anti-China Corporate Insurgency"

In the last section I showed that in the debate about US–China free trade in the early 1990s, organized labor and manufacturers that were initially reluctant to offshore constituted a coalition against unconditional renewal of China's MFN status. Ultimately, this coalition lost the battle to the coalition of high finance and influential corporations incentivized by Beijing's promises. After its defeat in 1994, the anti-China trade coalition lost energy when the disempowerment of labor unions in US politics accelerated and the initially reluctant manufacturers eventually offshored to China. Following China's accession to the WTO in 2001, the "China shock" to the US economy was immediate and vast. Between 1999 and 2001, the influx of Chinese imports accounted for the loss of more than two million manufacturing jobs in the United States (Acemoglu et al. 2016; Autor et al. 2016; Scott and Mokhiber 2018). This shock revitalized the anti-China trade coalition in the 2000s.

In less than five years after China's accession to the WTO, a lobbying coalition advocating designation of China as a currency manipulator emerged.

The designation of a trade partner as currency manipulator was enabled by a 1988 US law. A country's currency value against the USD is supposed to rise alongside its export increases to the United States. If a country's central bank intervenes to stem the appreciation of its currency, the undervalued currency would give its export sector protracted price competitiveness. Such central bank intervention is regarded as a nonmarket, unfair subsidy to the export sector at the expense of US manufacturers' market share and manufacturing jobs. In these circumstances, the law allows the US government to adopt remedial actions including placing extra duties on imports from that country or using government procurement rules to shun such imports. The purpose of the new anti-China trade coalition is to lobby Congress and the White House to designate China as a currency manipulator and adopt remedial measures to stem the influx of Chinese imports (see Blustein 2019: ch. 5).

The backbone of this coalition is organized labor. US manufacturers who turned out to be less capable of offshoring to China and are seeing their home market eroded by Chinese imports have joined the coalition as another formidable force. Most of these are from the steel industry, but they also include manufacturers of petrochemical products and precision equipment. Several umbrella organizations involved, or formed, to lobby Washington on the issue include the China Currency Coalition, the Alliance for American Manufacturing, the American Iron and Steel Institute, the Coalition for a Prosperous America, the Committee to Support US Trade Laws, and the Fair Currency Coalition.[4] The coalition's influence in Washington grew when unemployment brought about by manufacturing job losses attributable to China trade increased in the 2000s. It gained key allies among Congress members from the hard-hit areas, such as those from Midwestern Rust Belt represented by the "Congressional Steel Caucus." These areas have also become key battlegrounds in presidential elections.

While the China currency manipulation accusation climbed up the political agenda in Washington, thanks to the efforts of the coalition, it stopped short of succeeding in making the administration designate China as a currency manipulator and adopt the requested remedies – except for a brief moment of such designation in August 2019–January 2020 under the Trump administration. One reason for its lack of success is that these lobbying efforts had been countered by a countervailing lobbying coalition constituted by US corporations that have benefited from manufacturing outsourcing to China, and hence a low China currency. Such powerful counter-lobbyists include Walmart, Eastman Kodak, Caterpillar, Footwear Distributors and Retailers of America, National Retail

---

[4] For example, see Inside US Trade (2010).

Federation, American Electronic Association, the US–China Business Council, and some Wall Street banks.[5] They pointed out that the RMB has appreciated orderly since 2005, an appreciation that was regarded by the anti-China trade coalition as too little too late (see, e.g., Inside US Trade 2015a, 2015b, 2015c).

US corporations had been split on the question of China's currency manipulation and tariffs on Chinese imports in the 2000s. In the 2010s, more widespread reservation or even hostility toward China emerged among US corporations over the issues of intellectual property rights and market access. Whereas lobbying against China's alleged currency manipulation was initiated by corporations which could not outsource to China and resisted by corporations with a significant presence in China, the lobbying efforts concerning intellectual property rights protection and market access in China were spearheaded by US corporations with a significant presence in China.

For fear of retaliation by the Chinese government, many companies did not openly criticize the Chinese government's policy on technology transfer and market access. Instead, they clandestinely fed the US government information about their misgivings and lobbied Washington to take action on their behalf (Davis and Wei 2020a: 122). Some, however, did make their actions more public. For example, Micron Technology, a California-based memory chip manufacturer, filed a lawsuit in California against its Chinese competitor Jinhua, accusing it of masterminding a theft of its technology. After Jinhua countersued Micron in a Chinese court with the backing of the party–state and won, Micron leaned on its political connections to convince the US Department of Commerce that Jinhua's theft of its technology constituted a national security threat. In 2018, the Department of Commerce decided to backlist Jinhua and barred it from obtaining US technology and components, effectively bringing down the company (Davis and Wei 2020a: 265).

Besides technology transfer, restrictive market access constitutes another major issue where US corporations try to pressure Washington for assistance. Some US corporations started to complain, as early as 2004, that the Chinese government had not opened the Chinese market to them as widely as promised following China's accession to the WTO. Despite the subtle pressure exercised by the Bush and Obama administrations through behind-closed-door negotiations and WTO lawsuits, many practices and regulations that favored Chinese enterprises in their competition with foreign enterprises – such as uneven investigation and enforcement of anti-monopoly laws targeting foreign companies – continued to worsen after 2010 (US–China Business Council 2014).

---

[5] Based on my database compiled from the Congress lobbying disclosure database.

On January 19, 2011, when Obama held a joint press conference with Hu Jintao at the White House at the end of Hu's state visit, the Amercan president publicly raised the issue of unfair treatment of US corporations by Chinese authorities, albeit in diplomatic politeness, for the first time:

> I did also stress to President Hu that there has to be a level playing field for American companies competing in China, that trade has to be fair. So I welcomed his commitment that American companies will not be discriminated against when they compete for Chinese government procurement contracts. And I appreciate his willingness to take new steps to combat the theft of intellectual property (quoted in Reuters 2011).

Besides pressuring the White House, US corporations have also been active in lobbying Congress and urging it to take action against restrictive market access and intellectual property appropriation in China. As shown in Figure 8, business lobbying on the two issues rose steadily after 2004, peaked in 2010, and stayed at a high level thereafter.

While the lobbying activities surrounding currency manipulation show a split between US corporations, those concerning market access and intellectual property rights in China demonstrate a consensus among US corporations across different sectors. The list of corporations and organizations involved in lobbying Congress over these issues in 2019 – a peak year for such efforts – manifests a broad spectrum, including Oracle, IMB, Google, GM, Eli Lilly,

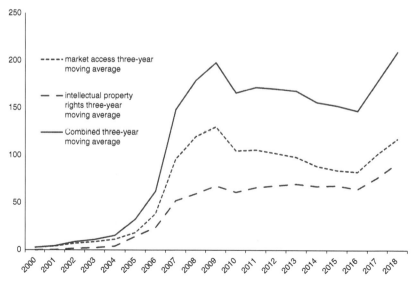

Figure 8 Count of US corporate lobbying involving China on intellectual property rights and market access, 1999–2019
Source: Secretary of Senate (n.d.).

National Chicken Council, Playboy, Morgan Stanley, United Steelworkers, and Conservatives for Property Rights.

Ultimately, the issues of market access, intellectual property rights, and even currency manipulation are all interrelated and can be seen as a manifestation of Beijing's general hostility toward US and other foreign companies. As early as January 2010, nineteen business lobbying groups including the Business Roundtable, the National Association of Manufacturers, and the US Chamber of Commerce wrote to the White House to complain about "[s]ystematic efforts by China to develop policies that build their domestic enterprises at the expense of US firms and US intellectual property" that "pose an immediate danger to U.S. companies," urging stronger action by Washington against China (cited in Meredith 2010). In 2017, the US Chamber of Commerce and the American Chamber of Commerce in China published *A Blueprint for Action: Addressing Priority Issues of Concern in U.S.–China Commercial Relations*. This was a list of demands for the new US administration regarding what it had to do to pressure Beijing to improve the business environment in China for US corporations. Its introduction succinctly summarizes the across-the-broad grievances of US corporations:

> Over the past several years, the business environment in China has deteriorated for many US and other foreign companies. This trend impacts companies not only operating in the country . . . . but also exporting into China and competing with Chinese companies in third-country markets . . . . It is essential that our future trade and investment strategy with China emphasize[s] the need for competitive markets in China, not merely defending our markets from subsidized steel and other commodities . . . . The substantial, growing, and harmful distortions of China industrial policies on the US and global economies will be far more damaging if China effectively eliminates foreign competition in its home market in critical areas ranging from electric vehicles to aviation to semiconductors. (US Chamber of Commerce and American Chamber of Commerce China 2017: 3)

Besides lobbying for China's designation as a currency manipulator, major labor organizations, including the AFL-CIO and the United Steelworkers, also earnestly lobby for pushback against China's policy of market access and technology transfer, asserting "the Chinese government cannot continue to violate international norms with respect to subsidies, investment, worker rights and trade policy – at the expense of American workers and producers" (AFL-CIO 2010).

Remarkably, some corporations that used to lobby on behalf of China's interests shifted their dispositions to lobbying for legislation against China. One notable example is Caterpillar, one of the key firms lobbying for China's

MFN status in the 1990s, when it started to establish itself in the Chinese market. In the early 2000s, it dominated China's construction machinery market. With the support of the financial stimulus of 2009–10, however, Chinese construction machine manufacturers expanded aggressively. China-made excavators' market share shot from 26 percent in 2009 to 62 percent in 2019, at the expense of Caterpillar's products, as well as European and Japanese machines (Dongxing Securities 2019: 8). Before 2010, Caterpillar openly lobbied against the Congressional bills that accused China of currency manipulation and approved US retaliatory tariffs on Chinese exports. After 2010, the company reversed its position. A stronger Chinese currency would benefit the company by boosting its exports to China while defending its US and other non-China markets from its Chinese competitors, which offer a product lineup that "suspiciously resembles" Caterpillar design (Hook 2013). A lobbyist for Caterpillar has noted that "[g]etting China to change its monetary policy is a huge issue and the US – from the government to businesses – is lobbying China to fix what they see as a major inequality that affects trade" (quoted in Wagreich 2013: 150).

The rise of an "anti-China corporate insurgency" (Wagreich 2013) was the force behind the Obama administration's redoubled effort to push for the Trans-Pacific Partnership (TPP) agreement. The idea of the TPP was to establish a free-trade zone, including the United States and most Asia-Pacific countries, except China. The TPP emphasized protecting intellectual property rights, guaranteeing market access, and restricting state-owned enterprises that are in competition with private ones. These are the issues that US corporations complain about most in China. The TPP, if realized, was expected to put pressure on China to improve its intellectual property protection and market access, as well as reduce government support for state-owned enterprises – all conditions for China to join the TPP. Such an "anti-China corporate insurgency" also supported Trump's tougher stance on China trade, and it underlines the continuation, and even hardening, of this tough stance into the Biden administration (Davis and Wei 2020b; Leary and Davis 2021).

3.4 Business Lobby and Geopolitical Pivot

At the height of "Chimerica," US corporations that enjoyed actual and expected benefits from the Chinese market have been China's "lobbyists by proxy." They not only lobbied for policies favorable to Chinese interests (e.g., the granting of Permanent Normal Trade Relation status to China), but also lobbied against any policy that would hurt Chinese interests. As a senior lobbyist in one of Washington's most coveted lobbying firms remarked: "The business community has always been the tip of the spear in terms of keeping the US–China relationship on a good track" (cited in Wagreich 2013: 151).

With US corporations becoming less enthusiastic about lobbying for China's interests, a key counterforce to Washington's more hawkish stance toward China disappeared. This unleashed the political forces advocating a tough policy on China in the national security arena, which had been checked by the pro-China corporate lobby. Geopolitical hawks in the US military–intelligence–diplomatic establishment had long warned of China's threat to US cybersecurity and US dominance in the Asia-Pacific. But every administration at the height of Chimerica has been wary of taking serious action to push back China's military and geopolitical advancement for fear of damaging US–China economic cooperation.

After 2010, hawkish geopolitical arguments became more influential in the policymaking process. One consequence was Obama's Pivot to Asia Policy, launched in 2011, that aimed to reallocate more naval power to the Pacific to counteract China's rising naval presence (Lieberthal 2011). In 2013, the US Navy began regular Freedom of Navigation operations in the South China Sea, sailing warships through waters crucial to global shipping but claimed by China as its maritime territories. Standoffs and confrontation between the US and Chinese navies became the new normal.

Once the national security hawks were unchecked and could dominate policymaking, Washington became more prone to adopt policy driven by the imperatives of geopolitical competition with China, even if it risked hurting the interests of particular US corporations. One of the most notable examples is the change in US policy toward Huawei, a Chinese private tech giant believed to have a close connection with the Chinese military and security apparatus. When Huawei climbed up the value chain and emerged as a global player in high-tech telecommunications, it established mutually beneficial relations with US tech companies. As a manufacturer of consumer telecom equipment and telecom infrastructure systems, Huawei relied on high-end computer chips and advanced components manufactured by US companies or high-tech firms in countries closely allied with the US, like Taiwan and South Korea, whose products rely on US-licensed technology. As a rising global giant tightly integrated with the US-dominanated high-tech supply chain, Huawei did not compete with most US firms, and instead became a major customer of US tech firms (Matsumoto and Watanabe 2020; Pham 2019).

When national security officials and Congress started to question Huawei's connection to the Chinese military and the cybersecurity risk arising from the telecom system it built in the US and allied countries, Washington initially downplayed those considerations. Indeed, it continued to support Huawei's expansion into the United States. The Bush administration was supportive of Huawei's entrance into the US market – it attempted to weaken the review power of the Committee on Foreign Investment in the United States (CFIUS) over Huawei to facilitate a merger of Huawei with a US company (Homeland Security News Wire 2007). In 2010, a former national security official from the Bush administration joined Huawei to advise on its business growth into the US market (Kirchgaessner 2010). This US–China tech cooperation continued into the early Obama years before taking a sharp turn.

In 2012, the White House and the House of Representatives reviewed the potential security risks posed by Huawei, leading Washington to bar US government offices from procuring from Huawei in 2013 (Menn 2012; Schmidt et al. 2012). In 2014, the National Security Agency launched an investigation into Huawei, which evoked a strong reaction by the Chinese government (Gokey 2014). Thus, a shift was underway in the early 2010s, when Washington turned from supporting cooperation with Huawei to forestalling it. It later evolved into a policy of pressuring US allies to ban Huawei from their telecommunication infrastructure and banning the export of US-made computer chips or computer chips carrying US technologies from around the world to Huawei. This aggressive policy against Huawei was devised by the Trump administration and it obtained bipartisan support in Congress. When the Trump White House attempted to ease its ban on selling equipment and components to Huawei in 2019 in anticipation of the beginning of US–China trade talks, and Beijing's concession in the talks, it provoked an immediate bipartisan pushback from Congress (Miller 2019). This aggressive policy was solely based on national security considerations. The fact that the policy could advance and take hold despite its damage to the interests of many American high-tech firms, which sold equipment, components, and technology to fuel Huawei's global expansion, showcases how much the structural conditions of US–China relations have changed.

The weakening of US corporate support for amicable US–China relations, as well as the receding of efforts to restrain the foreign policy elite, which prefers to position China as a US rival, came at a time when the popular backlash against globalization in general, and trade with China in particular, had reached a new height. Since the advent of neoliberal globalization and the opening of US–China free trade, organized labor and their political representatives have adamantly resisted these developments. Having experienced massive manufacturing offshoring and unemployment, as predicted by the critics of globalization in the early 1990s, downwardly mobile workers became a potent voting block that propelled anti-trade politicians – from Bernie Sanders on the left to Donald Trump on the right – to prominence in the 2016 presidential election.

Both Trump and Sanders saw unfettered free trade with China as a mistake. After Trump became President, he launched a trade war with China by leveling high tariffs against a wide range of Chinese products. The reservations about and even hostility toward China trade became so mainstream in Washington that even the new Biden administration pledged not to withdraw Trump's China tariffs and to continue pursuing a confrontational policy toward China.

4 Spheres of Influence

4.1 China's Rise as a Capital Exporter

As we saw in the last section, China's stimulus program in response to the 2008 global financial crisis successfully led to a rebound of the Chinese economy in 2009–10. However, the stimulus also led to an overaccumulation crisis characterized by rising indebtedness, excess capacity, and falling profits for Chinese enterprises. Under the weight of these problems, economic growth slowed after 2010, and this slowdown prompted the Chinese state to expand its control over the economy and redouble its squeeze on private and foreign enterprises. Another remedy for the toughening business environment in the domestic economy was the surge of capital exports in the form of FDI and external lending, as shown in Figure 9.

Although the amount of outward FDI far exceeds external loans, more than 70 percent of China's outward FDI, both in stock and flow, is directed to offshore financial centers including Hong Kong and Caribbean tax havens, and mostly ends up in holding companies and real estate in these centers,

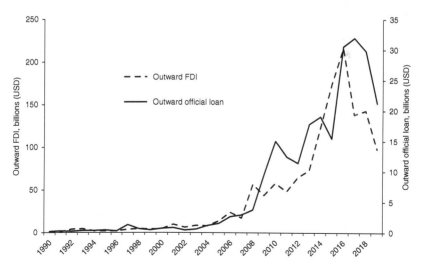

Figure 9 Annual disbursement of China's outward official loan and outward FDI, 1990–2019

Source: World Bank a (n.d.).

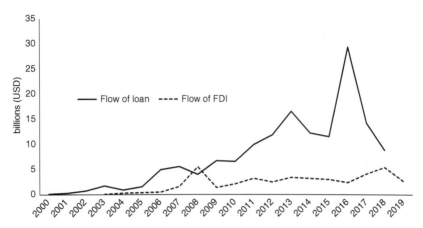

Figure 10 Annual flow of Chinese loan vs. Chinese FDI to Africa, 2000–19
Source: Ministry of Commerce, People's Republic of China (2010, 2015, 2019); JHU CARI (n.d.).

indicating that most of this investment is capital flight (Hung 2020c). In the case of Africa, where Chinese FDI data are least distorted by capital flight, loans always prevail over FDI as the main form of capital export (see Figure 10). Based on data in Africa, we could project that, discounting capital flight, China's foreign aid, mostly as loans offered by China's official financial institutions, has become the predominant form of its capital export to the developing world. Chinese external lending, on the aggregate level, has become comparable to direct lending by the United States and the World Bank (Horn et al. 2019: figures 4 and 5).

In the 2000s, amid the global commodity boom, many of China's loans to other developing countries allowed it to lock in raw materials from those countries (see Brautigam 2011). Many loans were made to energy or raw material exporting countries and repaid with specified amounts of commodities. The best-known example of this type of loan is China's $63 billion to Venezuela in 2007–14, to be repaid with oil deliveries (Balding 2017). After 2010, more loans went to finance infrastructure projects that paved the way for the export of China's overcapacity in infrastructure construction (Lyons 2021). Much of this capital export was put under the umbrella of the Belt and Road Initiative (BRI) from 2013. For Chinese-funded BRI projects, 89 percent of the projects' contractors were Chinese companies using Chinese materials, 7.6 percent were local companies, and 3.4 percent were non-Chinese foreign companies. In contrast, for projects funded by traditional multilateral institutions like the World Bank and the Asian Development Bank, 29 percent of contractors were

Chinese, 40.8 percent were local, and 30.2 percent were foreign (Hillman 2018).

This barrage of Chinese capital export to the developing world created new demands for Chinese enterprises struggling with overcapacity. For example, according to Chinese customs data, Chinese steel exports rose for more than twenty times between 2001 and a peak in 2015. Foreign sales created a lifeline for the many steel mills which expanded aggressively during the stimulus of 2009–10 and have been undermined by overcapacity and heavy debt ever since. Another sector plagued by excess capacity is construction machine manufacturing. Major construction machine manufacturers' capacity and revenue soared under the stimulus of 2009–10. But, as Figure 11 shows, the annual revenue change of the three major construction machine manufacturers in China plunged from a peak of robust growth in 2009–10 to contraction afterward, when the stimulus-induced rebound of the Chinese economy tapered off, and only started to grow again after 2013 with the beginning of the BRI Initiative. These companies' annual reports indicate the importance of orders from overseas Belt and Road projects, financed by Chinese lending, to their revenue growth compared with the stagnant domestic market (e.g., SANY n.d.; XGMC 2019)

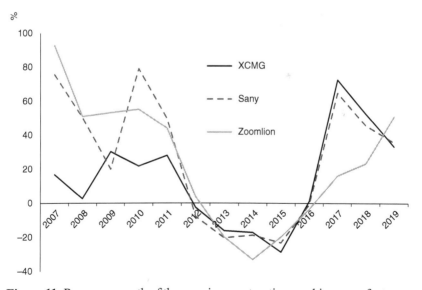

Figure 11 Revenue growth of three major construction machine manufacturers in China, 2007–19

Source: Company Financial Reports: XCMG (http://data.eastmoney.com/bbsj/yjbb/000425.html); Sany (https://data.eastmoney.com/bbsj/yjbb/600031.html); Zoomlion (http://data.eastmoney.com/bbsj/yjbb/000157.html).

As shown in the last section, party–state capitalism has increasingly protected domestic Chinese companies at the expense of US and other foreign companies in China's home market. China's capital export under the BRI created a Chinese sphere of influence in which Chinese goods and firms enjoyed privileged access vis-à-vis local firms and other foreign firms. In the last section, we saw that US corporations like construction machine makers have been losing market share in China to their state-supported Chinese competitors. But China's expanding influence in the developing world means that American corporations lose market there, too. Over the past decade, the global market share of Chinese construction machine manufacturers climbed rapidly at the expense of those in the United States. In 2020, China's Sany replaced Caterpillar for the first time as the top excavator seller in the world. Among the top ten construction machine manufacturers in the world (as of 2020), US companies (Caterpillar and John Deere) had a combined market share of 17.7 percent, whereas Chinese companies' (Sany, Zoomlion, and XCMG) combined market share is 20.3 percent (China Daily 2021; KHL 2021). It is not surprising, therefore, that US companies resorted to lobbying Washington for a policy that could enhance their competitiveness vis-à-vis their Chinese counterparts in the developing world. Caterpillar, for example, lobbied the Obama administration in 2011 for a free trade agreement with Colombia, explicitly stating the agreement was essential to boost its sales in the country and keep its Chinese competitors "at bay" (Inside US Trade 2011).

The 2017 action plan that the US Chamber of Commerce and AmCham China presented to the Trump administration explicitly protested that Chinese companies were exploiting the advantages they gained from US companies – through technology transfer, for example – to compete with US companies in the third-country market. A 2021 Council on Foreign Relations BRI taskforce, constituted of scholars and US business representatives, concludes that "BRI creates unfair advantages for Chinese companies, leaving U.S. and other foreign companies unable to compete in a number of BRI countries" (Lew et al. 2021: 22). Companies squeezed out by Chinese competitors in BRI countries named in the report include electronic payment companies like Paypal, construction contractors and engineering firms, and railroad equipment manufacturers in countries that are US allies, such as Germany and Japan. Thus, intercapitalist competition between US and Chinese corporations is not confined to China's domestic market – the competition has gone global.

4.2 New Dependency in the Global South

While China's capital export to other developing economies is to serve the need of its domestic political economy, the impact of China's inroads into other developing economies varies. Although China offers opportunities to develop-ing countries as a new, expanding market for commodities exports and as a source of capital, it also becomes a source of dependence for many developing countries.

Industrialization through reduced reliance on commodity exports has been a long-standing priority of many governments pursuing independent develop-ment. Developing countries have attempted to achieve this through import substitution (i.e., restraining imports of foreign manufactures to foster the growth of domestic industries) or export-oriented industrialization (subsidizing and promoting local industrial products for sale in the world market) (see Gallagher and Porzecanski 2010; Karl 1997; Shafer 1994). The rise of China has disrupted such endeavors in many developing countries.

Soaring Chinese demand for oil, raw materials, agricultural products, and many other commodities drove up global commodity prices and boosted the profits of commodity exporters (Roache 2012). And increased earnings in commodity-exporting countries led to the expansion of extractive industries and agribusiness, neutralizing development policies designed to reduce the share of commodity exports in their economies. For example, the amount of land used for soybean cultivation in Brazil doubled between 1990 and 2005. This entailed the expansion of farmland deep into the environmentally sensitive Amazon frontier. This vast expansion was largely driven by China's demand, which constituted 42.7 percent of Brazil's soybean exports in the early 2000s. The share shot up to 80 percent in 2018 amid the US–China trade war that drove more Chinese importers to turn to Brazil. In Argentina, Chinese companies dominated both ends of the soybean commodity chain, skewing the economy's distribution of income even more than is usually the case when integrated commodity chains serve markets in developed countries (Sly 2017).

The copper mining industries in Chile and other Latin American countries also expanded significantly during the same period; exports of copper from Latin America increased by 237.5 percent between 2000 and 2006. Most of this increased production went to China. In 2016, 67 percent of Chile's copper exports and 73 percent of Peru's exports were to China (Gallagher and Porzecanski 2010: 22, passim; Gonzalez 2018). Much of the same phenomenon occurred in Africa, where countries rich in metal ores, such as Zambia, saw the boom of their extractive sectors, with China becoming their main market, though China's recent slowdown hit their raw materials exports (Wang 2017).

Although China helps boost raw material sectors, its efficient, low-cost industries put increasing pressure on manufacturing sectors across the develop-ing world. Some argue that the genesis of China's export-oriented manufactur-ing in the 1990s, particularly after the one-off devaluation in 1994 of China's currency (the RMB) to boost exports, is responsible for the economic troubles of other Asian exporters, like Malaysia and Thailand, and that it paved the way for the Asian financial crisis of 1997–8 (e.g., Krause 1998). Chinese manufactured exports created similar pressure on Latin American industries, especially in Mexico (Gallagher and Porzecaski 2010: 50).

The combined effect of expanding raw material export sectors and increasing competitive pressures on domestic industries resulting from the China boom created conditions for deindustrialization and the return of dependence on exports of natural resources in the developing world. Whether or how much this change will damage or benefit the long-term developmental prospects of individual developing countries, and whether it will bring about the so-called "resource curse", depends on each country's internal political economy.

The mining sector in many Latin American countries is dominated by state companies or heavily regulated by the government, allowing these countries to have some leverage over pricing and output in their negotiations with China and also enabling them to put mining profits into more productive investments. In contrast, most African countries lack competitive homegrown mining corporations and rely on foreign companies to extract their resources (Anderson 2011; Jepson 2020). In many cases, Chinese state companies, often in tacit partnership with other transnational mining corporations, own and run the entire commodity chain from mining sites to the ports that ship the raw materials. African governments are in a much less favorable position to negotiate with their Chinese partners, and the latter can concentrate on maximizing short-term gains without considering the long-term impact on the local economy, society, and environment (Haglung 2019; Lee 2017).

The 2009-10 stimulus in China led to a domestic infrastructure construction boom. This created a surge in global demand for commodities that benefited commodity exporters across the developing world (Jepson 2020). Demand from China was the main reason many of these exporters, from Brazil to Zambia, were spared from the worst effects of the global financial crisis in 2008. When China's construction boom fizzled out after 2010, its demand for commodities fell and many commodity exporters, buoyed by the China boom, experienced a slowdown or even recession. The economic crises in Brazil and Venezuela in the 2010s are cases in point. Simultaneously, the Chinese economy started to be plagued by overcapacity and an economic slowdown. as we saw in the previous section. In this context, making developmental loans to other developing countries to finance infrastructure projects, which then hired Chinese contractors and procured Chinese materials, became an increasingly significant form of China's capital export (Horn et al. 2019).

A country's increasing indebtedness to China usually brings a large trade deficit. One example is Pakistan, which, according to World Bank data, borrowed heavily from China after 2010 to fund the port and road projects linked to the China–Pakistan Economic Corridor (CPEC) and owned the largest stock of Chinese official loans as of 2019. Corresponding to the surge in Chinese loans was Pakistan's rising imports of machinery and construction materials from China. Pakistan's trade deficit with China soared. In 2018, Pakistan plunged into a balance of payments and currency crisis that pushed the government to seek an emergency loan from the IMF. Many attributed the crisis to Pakistan's deep involvement in the debt-driven CPEC with China (Runde and Olson 2018).

Besides the trade deficit resulting from Chinese loans, the sustainability of the debt-driven infrastructure boom is another concern. China's infrastructure lending to the developing world is an externalization of its domestic stimulus program in 2009–10, when Chinese state banks opened the flood gates of loans to fund local governments and state enterprises so they could pursue fixed-asset investment. As most of these investments fed industrial overcapacity and were not going to be profitable, the loans were unsustainable and led to a debt time bomb among local governments and state enterprises (Hung 2016: ch. 3). While the Chinese government could contain the domestic debt crisis by bailing out state-sector debtors on the verge of defaulting through loan rollovers, write-off, or fiscal injections (Kauko 2020; Koons 2013), this remedy is infeasible for China's external debtors in the developing world. In light of the default risk, many Chinese external loans contained conditions about collaterals, allowing China to seize control of strategic facilities in case of default. For example, the Sri Lankan government started to borrow from China and hire Chinese contractors to build a new port in the strategic coastal city of Hambantota, which oversees a busy shipping lane in the Indian Ocean. The port continuously lost money after it opened in 2010. The Sri Lankan government eventually defaulted on the loan and let the Chinese state-owned operator seize control of the port on a ninety-nine-year lease in 2017 (Frayer 2019).

It is still too early to know whether the case of Hambantota is an exception or the rule, but it has already raised alarm and invoked debate about whether the Chinese loans were set up in a way that would make repayment difficult, if not impossible, and whether Beijing's real intention was to create dependency on Chinese finance and seize control of strategic facilities across the developing world using its loans (Kazeem 2020; cf. Brautigam 2020; Gelpern et al. 2021). As many of those strategic facilities would be located at geopolitical choke points, some speculate that they would eventually become springboards for China's projection of military power far from home. This leads us to ponder the geopolitical implications of China's capital exports, which are turning China into a new imperial power.

4.3 Late Imperialism and Its Discontents

When China's economic power in Asia and beyond increases, Beijing will naturally try to leverage its economic clout to increase its geopolitical influence. The way Beijing acts vis-à-vis its Asian neighbors could be a harbinger of how it will interact with other regions. China's imperial turn – as the projection of a state's formal or informal political power beyond its sovereign border – is hardly surprising.

China's economic rise and the end of the Cold War made it possible to pursue a new Sinocentric order with incumbent governments in Asia that resemble the premodern Sinocentric order (Hamashita 2008; Kang 2010). As both rich and poor Asian countries become more integrated with the Sinocentric production network and grow dependent on Chinese investment and loans, many already see that Beijing has been using threats to curtail economic ties as a diplomatic weapon. For example, China is rarely hesitant to use or threaten to use economic leverage to reinforce its territorial claims in disputes with Southeast Asian nations and Japan. But the continuous engagement of the United States in the region enables other Asian nations to counterbalance China's economic and political influence. The swing between partial democracy and military dictatorship, and the fluctuation of Myanmar between the United States and China, is partly a result of US–China competition over the region. (Bower 2010; Mandhana et al. 2021; O'Connor 2011).

Singapore, South Korea, the Philippines, Taiwan, Vietnam, and many other Asian states have also bolstered their economic and political–military ties with the United States at the same time as they are benefiting from increased economic integration with China. These Asian states have become a battleground where China and the United States are competing for influence. Similar dynamics can also be seen in South Asia and Central Asia. For example, in the 2015 presidential election in Sri Lanka, the challenger, Maithripala Sirisena, ran on an anti-China platform and defeated the two-term incumbent, Mahinda Rajapaksa, who had approved many large infrastructure projects to be built and financed by China. After the election, many Chinese projects were delayed or revisited by the new government. In the 2019 presidential election and 2020 parliamentary election, Mahinda Rajapaksa and his brother won back power. It is expected that Sri Lanka will tilt back toward China as China-backed projects regain momentum (Sala 2017; Shah and Jayasinghe 2020).

In Pakistan, many regional elites see Chinese projects as enabling the central military elite to tighten its grip on their regions and resources (Hameed 2018). These projects, as well as the Chinese personnel involved, became the targets of local rebel groups. In 2017, Pakistan's government canceled the Chinese-financed $14 billion Diamer-Bhasha Dam project, citing harsh loan terms that involved pledging the new dam and an existing dam as loan security. Pakistan then turned to the IMF for emergency loans to deal with the balance of payment crisis that the CPEC helped precipitate. In response, the IMF asked Pakistan "to reduce trade and commerce reliance on Beijing" as a condition for the loan (Kahn 2020).

In 2017, Nepal canceled a $2.5 billion contract with Gezhouba Group, a Chinese company, for the construction of a hydroelectric plant. The government cited irregularities and corruption during the bidding process. In 2018, the Malaysian opposition ran on an anti-corruption platform, accusing the incumbent government of collaborating with China through the BRI and that this damaged Malaysia's national interests. Surprisingly, the opposition won the election and renegotiated many of the major Belt and Road projects with China after it took power (Parameswaran 2019; Radio Free Asia 2019). The Philippines populist President Duterte, who constantly threatened to sever military ties with the United States and shifted allegiance to China, could not withstand domestic pressure and took a firmer stance by denying China's sovereignty claim in their territorial dispute (Strangio 2020).

Beijing's efforts to expand its geopolitical influence by leveraging its rising economic dominance are not confined to Asia. Africa is another region where China's influence has been growing rapidly (Brautigam 2011). Many African states carefully maintained good relations with China by supporting Beijing's position on political issues such as Taiwan's status and visits by the Dalai Lama. However, concern about "Chinese colonialism" started to emerge within Africa when labor disputes sometimes turned bloody and corruption charges involving Chinese companies increased. Opposition parties across the continent began to take advantage of the popular resentment against China's inroads by attacking incumbent governments for meeting China's demands at the expense of local interests. In the 2011 election in Zambia, the opposition party campaigned on an anti-China platform and successfully ousted the incumbent party (French 2011).

Concern about China's growing influence in Africa has reached a point where sitting governments that have a close relationship with China feel compelled to address this issue. In March 2013, just before the BRICS summit in Durban, the then governor of the Central Bank of Nigeria, one of the African countries that has been most heavily reliant on Chinese loans, warned in the *Financial Times* that by embracing China, Africa is "opening itself up to a new form of imperialism ... China takes from us primary goods and sells us manufactured ones. This was also the essence of colonialism" (Sanusi 2013).

Similar dynamics are at work in Latin America. The improvement in relations between the United States and Brazil during the Obama administration illustrates this dynamic. Brazil benefited significantly from the resource bonanza driven by Chinese demand, but at a substantial cost to the environment. The industrialist backlash against China's alleged mercantilist trade and currency policies has checked its influence in Brazil, which supported Washington's accusation of China's currency manipulation at the WTO (Dalton and Kinch 2011). How the 2018 victory of Jair Bolsonaro, who accused China of buying up Brazil and identified it as a national security threat, will shape Brazil–China relations remains to be seen. In the general election in Peru in 2021, the hard-left candidate Pedro Castillo closely won on a platform that cast foreign mining companies, mostly Chinese, as neocolonial and called for the renegotiation of mining rights with foreign companies and for levying new taxes on them.

Even Latin American countries once considered reliable allies of Beijing now sometimes act against Beijing's wishes. Venezuela is one such example. When the late socialist president Hugo Chavez broke with the United States – the principal consumer of Venezuelan oil – he turned to China as an alternative market and source of political support. Beijing provided the aforementioned loan-for-oil deal. When Venezuela's economy fell into deep crisis amid falling oil prices, the government of Chavez's successor, Nicholas Maduro, began to delay shipments of oil that were earmarked for loan repayment and, instead, to sell the oil in international markets for cash. Many Chinese companies subsequently left Venezuela without finishing their construction projects. When Maduro had difficulty securing more Chinese loans, he started turning to Wall Street again for credit in 2017 (Vyas and Kurmanaev 2017; Wernau 2018).

These challenges have constrained China's economic expansion into the developing world. China's export of capital and goods to the Belt and Road countries surged dramatically after Xi Jinping announced it as his pet project. But the growth of China's capital exports declined significantly from 2016, as shown in the outward FDI and loans data in Figure 9 (see also Niewenhuis 2020). The bottleneck for China's ambitious attempts to become a major capital exporter with an extensive sphere of influence is as much geopolitical as it is financial. Developing countries receiving Chinese investment and loans always had the United States and other great powers (such as India, in the case of Sri Lanka and Nepal) to fall back on. This has checked China's expanding influence. For China to overcome this bottleneck, it will have to overcome US dominance in the global financial and geopolitical order.

4.4 Challenging the US Empire

So long as the global dollar standard, the Bretton Woods multilateral organizations, and the US global military umbrella remain dominant, China's projection of its geopolitical influence will be constrained. Countries that China tried to absorb into its own orbit could often count on the United States to check China's growing influence. Beijing was well aware of this obstacle, and it has started exploring ways to create a parallel global currency system, multilateral institutions, and even security–military hard power to rival the United States.

The rise of China as an export-oriented manufacturing powerhouse hinges its dependence on the USD. China's exports are almost totally invoiced in USD, just like Japan and the Four Tigers before it (Hung 2016: ch. 5), and its payments for imports are also in USD. Its recycling of its foreign exchange reserves (mostly in USD) in US Treasury bonds help sustain the global dollar standard and the US-led global financial architecture. The global financial crisis that started in the US in 2008 and heavily damaged the USD's credibility urged China to rethink its dependence on the dollar.

Starting in 2008, China promoted the international use of the RMB, hoping that China's external trade and its investment inflow and outflow could increasingly be settled in RMB instead of the dollar. The biggest challenge to the RMB's internationalization is that it is not a freely convertible currency, as the CCP never lets go of its control over the financial system to liberalize China's capital account. The RMB's inconvertibility dampens its global demand. Beijing's remedy was to promise eventual free convertibility of the RMB, while building up a freely convertible offshore RMB market in Hong Kong (Hung In press: ch. 3). International use of the RMB appeared to increase significantly in the years following the 2008 global financial crisis, though it was still trailing far behind international use of the euro, let alone the USD. The financial meltdown and drastic depreciation of the RMB in China in 2015, resulting from China's economic slowdown, overcapacity, and debt bubble as discussed in the last section, forced Beijing to tighten foreign exchange control again to stem capital flight. In the aftermath of the turmoil, Beijing prioritized financial stabilization and put RMB internationalization on the back burner. Today, most of China's trade and outward investment are still denominated in USD, as, overwhelmingly, are its external loans (as shown in Figure 12) (see also Horn et al. 2019).

Beijing's attempt to create an RMB currency bloc to reduce its dependence on the USD has so far been futile. But its aggressive push for RMB internationalization in the aftermath of the global financial crisis in 2008 did reveal China's

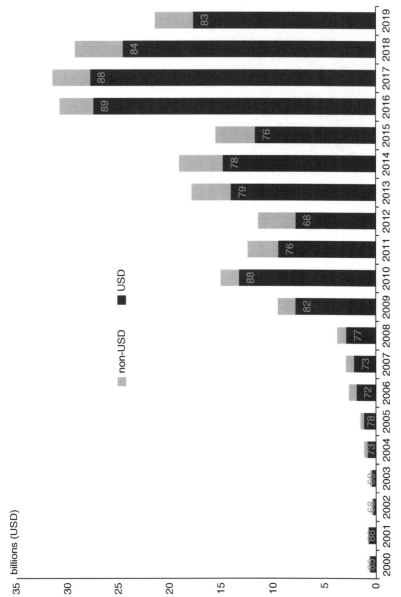

Figure 12 Currency denomination of China's public external lending (numbers denote USD %).
Source: World Bank b (n.d.).

intention of challenging USD hegemony. This intention kept the United States alert. In 2019, a US Congress report claimed that RMB internationalization still maintains a certain momentum. This, in combination with the creation and rapid growth of the Cross-Border Interbank Payments System (CIPS), a China-led international clearing system independent of the US-led SWIFT (Society for Worldwide Interbank Financial Telecommunications), could potentially create a China-led global financial system to challenge the US-led system. This financial system could become a lifeline for countries subject to US sanctions, including North Korea, Syria, Russia, and Iran (US–China Economic and Security Review Commission 2019).

Besides attempting to set up a parallel global currency system, Beijing strives to reduce the backlash against its bilateral economic inroads into other developing countries by setting up its own multilateral institutions. These could provide a multilateral cover to China's economic expansion into the developing world. The creation of the Asian Infrastructure Investment Bank (AIIB) in spring 2015 to finance infrastructure projects in Central, South, and Southeast Asia is a significant step in this approach. As of December 2017, the bank had seventy members, forty-four from within and twenty-six from outside the Asian region, including some European countries. AIIB capitalization can potentially go up to $100 billion; China's pledged contribution is $50 billion. By the end of 2019, however, the total loans that AIIB had committed to and disbursed over the four years of its existence amounted to only $8.4 billion and $2.9 billion, respectively (AIIB 2020) – far short of the initial expectation of an annual loan disbursement of $10–15 billion per year.[6] With the Obama administration's decision to boycott the AIIB, the competition between the United States and China over multilateral lending to the developing world became apparent (Wu 2016). While refusing to join the AIIB, the United States established the International Development Finance Corporation in 2018, with an exposure cap of $60 billion as a response to the AIIB (Congressional Research Service 2019).

If China's bilateral developmental assistance had been working well, it would not have needed to build new multilateral banks. China can lend alone, which allows it to maintain total control over which counttries to lend to and the terms of the loans. Lending through multilateral banks like AIIB constrains China's freedom of action because other stakeholders also have a say, despite China's veto power. Moreover, even though China is the largest contributor to the AIIB, it is still subject to the standards of existing multilateral lending institutions.

---

[6] Based on the AIIB website, as of March 6, 2018. www.aiib.org/en/about-aiib/governance/mem bers-of-bank/index.html.

China's efforts to start or support these multilateral institutions are attempts to diversify the risks of extending loans to other developing countries by sacrificing some of its power in dictating the terms of the loans (Hung 2015).

In contrast to speculation that the AIIB would become a vehicle to promote the international use of the RMB at the expense of the USD, the AIIB has little choice but to denominate the overwhelming majority of its loans in USD, as the demand for RMB loans is still minimal (Horn et al. 2019; Strohecker 2019). While the total amount of committed and disbursed loans made by the AIIB has been far short of initial expectations, most of the loans have been in partnership with US-led multilateral institutions like the World Bank and the Asian Development Bank as colenders (AIIB 2020). In this cofinancing with traditional multilateral banks, the AIIB relies on the traditional banks' expertise in assessing and shouldering the risks of its financed projects.

Another challenge to China's attempt to project its influence to other developing countries is the inherent security risk and greater engagement cost. As more Chinese funds, personnel, and critical production facilities are distributed among developing countries, many of them unstable and ruled by unpopular regimes, Beijing faces increasing pressure to protect them. Thus, the sabotage of Chinese facilities and kidnapping of Chinese personnel in unstable areas has grown more frequent. Chinese nationals have reportedly become the number one target for kidnapping by terrorists and rebel groups in Africa, and Chinese facilities are valuable targets for ransom demands (ENR 2014; NYA International 2015). Militant and terrorist groups who see the Chinese inroads as a new imperialist incursion also target Chinese personnel and facilities for political reasons (Kelemen 2019). The deadly attack by radical militants on the Chinese consulate in Karachi in 2018 was a case in point (Yousufzai 2020).

Since 2013, Beijing has pledged to deploy the People's Liberation Army (PLA) to protect its "core interests" overseas (Hung 2016: ch. 5). So far, the PLA's overseas operations have mostly been through its participation in UN peacekeeping. The PLA also started to follow the examples of the United States, the UK, and France in stationing a force in Djibouti to help patrol the transportation chokepoint connecting the Red Sea and the Arabian Sea, which is essential for international trade. But compared to the United States, Europe, and Russia, China's foreign direct military involvement is still minuscule.

To make up for the lack of military projection capability, Beijing has been experimenting with international mercenaries to defend its overseas interests. In 2014, Erik Prince, the founder and former CEO of Blackwater, the security firm that became infamous for its actions in Iraq, was recruited to head the Frontier Services Group (FSG), a new Hong Kong based logistics and security firm as a subsidiary to CITIC, China's biggest state-owned conglomerate. The FSG's main business is to provide security services to Chinese companies in Africa through a network of security subcontractors on the ground. In late 2016, the company announced that it was to adjust its corporate strategy to "better capitalize on the opportunities available from China's One Belt, One Road (OBOR) development initiative" (Frontier Services Group 2017). The FSG has been operating a large security training center in Beijing since 2017 and started building another one in Xinjiang in early 2019 (Reuters 2019). China's cooperation with Erik Prince to establish the FSG is probably not intended to be a long-term solution for the protection of Beijing's overseas interests, but it addresses an immediate and growing need. China has already started developing its own security companies to provide services to Chinese entities overseas without the help of foreigners like Erik Prince. Some examples include the China Security and Protection Group, HuaXin ZhongAn, Beijing DeWe Security Services Limited Company, and China Overseas Security Group (Nouwens 2018; Zheng 2019).

China's rise as a capital exporter follows in the footsteps of other capitalist powers in history, which went abroad for economic reasons before finding the necessity to project their political and military power beyond their own sovereign space to protect overseas economic interests. What China is doing is not novel – it is the path of informal imperialist expansion that, historically, many developed countries have followed. It is ironic that, just as many Western scholars sympathetic to China deny the notion that China has gone imperial, since at least 2004 CCP leaders have started becoming more frank about China's imperative to learn about global power projections from historic imperial powers since the fifteenth century including Spain, the Netherlands, the UK, France, and the United States (zhongguo qingnian bao 2006). More recently, an influential official scholar of China with significant policy influence explicitly wrote that China should "absorb the skills and achievements" of the British and American empires to construct its own "world empire" for the sake of the Chinese people and the world (Jiang 2019).

China's imperial turn fuels the growing anxiety of existing imperial powers, most of all the United States. It also worries many developing countries, which see increasing Chinese influence as a menace to their independent development and sovereignty. All developing countries that are experiencing expanding Chinese influence are now contemplating how to avoid the crossfire of the intensifying US–China rivalry. They also strive to benefit from such competition. Many countries see China's aid and investment as a viable counterbalance to preexisting US influences, and vice versa. They frequently play China and the United States against each other. It is the typical dynamic of interimperial rivalry that we saw in the last century.

5 Conclusion: Interimperial Rivalry Redux

In the aftermath of the Cold War, some saw the world as heading toward a "clash of civilizations" between established Western powers and the rising economic and demographic powers in the Sino and Muslim worlds (Huntington 1996). Some, on the other hand, saw the world as moving toward greater universal peace, unified under liberal democracy and free markets (Fukuyama 1992). Others saw the rise of a universal global capitalist empire, in which major capitalist powers united to dominate and carve up the world (Hardt and Negri 2000).

But this debate is by no means new – the history of capitalism is rife with war and conflict. Since the inception of capitalist modernity, there has been discussion about whether it would ultimately lead us to perpetual peace or great wars among major capitalist powers. We see the same debate at the turn of the twentieth century when the world saw an established capitalist power, the UK, facing intensifying challenges from rising latecomers – Germany and Japan. For Karl Kautsky (1914), the end of Pax Britannica and the rise of new capitalist powers toward the end of the nineteenth century would not necessarily lead to conflict. Kautsky put forward a theory of "ultra-imperialism," seeing that great capitalist powers could establish a joint cartel to divide and dominate the world together. The Scramble for Africa in the Berlin Congress in 1878 and the joint imperialist invasion of China by great powers in 1900 can be seen as ultra-imperialism in action. Under this ultra-imperialist formation, great powers could be at peace with one another for a long time.

Disagreeing with this prognosis, Lenin (1963 [1917]), building on the analysis of British economist J. A. Hobson, argued that great powers, when seeking to dominate the world through imperialist expansion, were destined to clash with one another. Any synergy among the great powers would, at most, be a temporary truce in between conflicts. Given the uneven pace of capitalist development among great powers, the division of the world based on the balance of power among those powers at any given point would certainly become outdated when the balance changed. This changing balance of power inevitably encouraged some powers to seek a redistribution of resources, which would inevitably lead to conflict. In the end, the two world wars vindicated Lenin's theory about the inevitability of great power conflict over Kautsky's theory of ultra-imperialist peace.

While the configuration of the world order following the end of the Cold War is still in flux, the rise of US–China symbiosis in the 1990s, and its replacement by a US–China rivalry in more recent years, lead many to question whether the two greatest world powers are heading toward war or whether they will revert to a more harmonious relationship. In this Element, I have borrowed insights from both Marxian and Weberian perspectives on international politics to unveil the economic and geopolitical origins of US–China symbiosis around 1990–2010 and US–China rivalry after c. 2010.

We saw in Section 2 that, since the 1970s, US corporations have been pushing for globalization as a remedy for their profitability crisis. In the early 1990s, they advocated for trade liberalization with China despite the foreign policy elite's tendency to see China as a new rival in the post–Cold War world. US corporate efforts to lobby for US–China trade liberalization in the early 1990s stemmed largely from Beijing's efforts to mobilize US companies and turn them into its proxy lobbyists. This trade liberalization paved the way for China's accession to the WTO in 2001, heralding the heyday of Chimerica in the early 2000s.

Over the 1990s, many of the foreign policy elite in the United States saw the prospect of conflict with China. Skirmishes between China and US allies in the South China Sea increased, concern about China's contribution to nuclear proliferation in North Korea and Pakistan rose, and the notion that authoritarian China posed a threat to US supremacy in Asia took hold. A "great power competition" between an established power and a rising power, *à la* Allison's Thucydides' trap, seemed to be emerging. Yet, in reality, general relations between the two countries continued to improve, as the Wall Street-led corporate sector worked hard to foster a more amicable relationship with China. This development in US–China relations in the 1990s shows the limits of the Thucydides' trap thesis, which overlooks the significance of transnational economic linkages. Into the 2000s, US preoccupation with the War on Terror in Central and West Asia encouraged the foreign policy elite in Washington to seek a more cooperative relationship with Beijing on East Asian security. The alignment of corporate and geopolitical interests on the side of amity consolidated the Chimerica formation.

At the apogee of the US–China symbiosis, cleavages between US corporations and China began to form. As US corporate presence in China increased, so did intellectual property infringement cases and complaints about China's unfulfilled promises of market access. Initially, these conflicts were more or less contained. As we saw in Section 3, the business environment that US corporations faced in China deteriorated significantly in the aftermath of the 2008 global financial crisis and Beijing's mega monetary stimulus of the state sector in 2009–10. Chinese enterprises faced an overcapacity and profitability crisis after the stimulus tapered off. With state regulatory and financial support, Chinese enterprises became more aggressive in appropriating technology and US corporations' market share in the Chinese market. This turned many US

Table 4 Foreign policy elite and corporations' disposition to US–China relations.

		Foreign policy elite disposition (Weberian geopolitical interests)	
Corporations'		Partner	Rival
disposition (Marxian	Partner	2000s US–China	1990s US–China
economic interests)	Rival	US–Europe	2010s US–China

companies, which used to be proxy lobbyists for Chinese interests, into lobbyists for a more assertive policy against China. They were, at least, no longer eager to neutralize any confrontational policies originating from the foreign policy elite, which turned its attention back to US competition with China in the West Pacific once the United States had exonerated itself from the War on Terror in the 2010s. Increasing US–China intercapitalist competition in the Chinese market eventually aligned US corporate dispositions toward China with that of the foreign policy elite on the side of enmity.

The changing alignment of US corporate and geopolitical interests regarding China is summarized in Table 4. There is not a period in which US corporations compete with their Chinese counterparts while the United States is China's geopolitical ally (bottom row, left). We could put the US–Europe or the US–Japan relation there as a substitute. US corporations always saw European and Japanese corporations as competitors, even as the United States was in a formal alliance with Europe and Japan under NATO and the US–Japan Security Pact. Table 4 shows that while US geopolitical interests have conflicted with China's most of the time, US corporate interests vary. Only when corporate and geopolitical interests align on the side of enmity does Washington turn to a more antagonistic posture toward China. Varying US corporate interests in China are, in turn, a result of China's changing political economy. Both the economic interests of capital (as definied from a Marxian perspective) and the geopolitical interests of the state (as defined from a Weberian perspective) are significant in shaping the US–China relationship.

We saw in Section 4 that besides squeezing foreign enterprises in the domestic market, Chinese enterprises also sought to overcome their overcapacity through exporting excess capital to other countries with state support. China's desire to export capital underlines the inception of the BRI. This initiative offered Chinese goods and contractors a vast new market. Chinese companies' competition with US corporations extended into BRI countries, many of whom had traditionally been US allies. China must now project its geopolitical power to protect Chinese investments abroad. In creating its sphere of influence at the expense of that of the United States, China clashed head-on with the latter as an established geopolitical power.

In sum, the combined and uneven development of US and Chinese capitalism led to intercapitalist competition between the two countries. This competition unleashed Washington's tendency to posit China as a geopolitical opponent, ripping apart the Chimerica formation and bringing about US–China rivalry in Asia and beyond. This intensifying US–China rivalry resembles the conflict between the UK and Germany in the early twentieth century, as Lenin discussed. At the turn of the twentieth century, Germany became a major capitalist power searching for overseas markets and outlets for its capital export. As it did not have many formal colonies like those of the UK, German capital export was led not by foreign direct investment but by German bank loans to support infrastructure projects – predominantly railroad construction – in Central and Southern Europe and Latin America, among other places. Borrowers of German loans were obliged to procure German products for their projects. German bankers competed with British and French banks in lending to central Europe and Latin America (Bersch and Kaminsky 2008; Lenin 1963 [1917]: 228; Young 1992). One such German-supported infrastructure project serving German business interests and geopolitical ambitions was the Berlin–Baghdad railroad proposed by Wilhelm II. The project connected Germany, the Austro–Hungarian Empire, and the Ottoman Empire and cut into British and Russian spheres of influence in the Near East, which became an increasingly important energy source when the world was transforming from coal to oil. The railroad also put Serbia at the epicenter of interimperial rivalry, contributing significantly to the outbreak of World War I (Kennedy 1980; Lenin 1963 [1917]: 223, 261; McMeekin 2012). *China*

After World War I, Germany tried to internationalize its currency, the Reichsmark, in Central and Southern Europe to facilitate the export of German capital by increasing the use of Reichmarks and creating a Reichsmarks bloc among those countries at the expense of the British pound (Milward 1985). This intensified UK and German competition over Central and Eastern Europe, first in the financial–monetary sphere and then in the political and military sphere. This policy resembles Beijing's attempt to internationalize the RMB and create an RMB economic bloc at the expense of the USD.

The precedent of intercapitalist competition turning into interimperial rivalry between the UK and Germany suggests that rivalry between the US and China is more likely to escalate than not, maybe even leading to war. Many observers have already noticed the comparability of China's sovereignty claims over areas controlled by US allies (Senkaku/Diaoyu Islands, South China Sea, Taiwan, etc.) to Germany's irredentism in the early twentieth century (e.g., Roy 2019). It is noteworthy that many influential official scholars in China have openly compared China's foreign policy agenda of "great revival" to Germany's position just a century earlier. Works of German statist thinkers like the Nazi jurist Carl Schmitt became popular among prominent scholar–officials in Beijing who have the ears of party–state leaders (Chang 2020; Qi 2012). The clash between China, as a rising empire, and the United States, an established one, looks increasingly like the Germany–UK conflict in the early twentieth century.

The comparability between the US–China conflict today and the UK–Germany conflict a century earlier does not mean that war is inevitable. What is different in the twenty-first century is that now there are various global governing institutions over which the United States, China, and their allies could struggle for influence and so resolve their conflicts instead of settling scores through war. These struggles have already started: US–China competition over influence in the UN, the WTO, the World Health Organization, and other institutions has been growing over the last decade.

Moreover, as Hobson points out, capitalist powers need to export capital in search of overseas profits when they fail to secure the higher incomes, and hence purchasing power, of the working class at home; this is necessary to absorb the excess productive capacity in their domestic economies (Hobson 2018 [1902]: ch. IV). If domestic redistribution advances, the capitalist powers would have less need to export capital, and hence a reduced incentive to carve out their sphere of influence and thus collide with other powers. In China's context, if Beijing's attempts to rebalance the economy by boosting household incomes and household consumption succeed, the Chinese political economy's overcapacity, profitability crisis, and indebtedness would be alleviated (Klein and Pettis 2020). Chinese enterprises, and the Chinese state behind them, would have less incentive to squeeze foreign companies in China. They would be less prone to overseas investment too. Reviving profits through redistribution instead of intensifying zero-sum intercapitalist competition could contain the deterioration into interstate conflict. The same applies to the redistributive reform vs. capital export through the pursuit of neoliberal globalization in the United States. Hobson's remedy for the avoidance of trade war, imperial expansion, and hence interimperial war more than a century ago still applies today:

> It is this economic condition of affairs [of excessive capital and productive capacity] that forms the taproot of Imperialism. If the consuming public in this country [UK] raised its standard of consumption to keep pace with every rise of productive powers, there could be no excess of goods or capital clamorous to use Imperialism in order to find markets: foreign trade would

indeed exist, but there would be no difficulty in exchanging a small surplus of our manufactures ... and all the savings that we made could find employment, if we chose, in home industries. (Hobson 2018 [1902]: 58)

To be sure, such a rebalancing act, which hinges on breaking the corporate oligarchies' resistance to redistribution, is easier said than done. Based on our theoretical understanding of China's capitalist development and US political economy, combined with a comparison with historical precedent, we are certain that the US–China rivalry will only intensify in the years to come. Mediation by legitimate global governing institutions and the rebalancing of the Chinese and American economies are two approaches that could help alleviate the conflict. Only time will tell whether such approaches will succeed and whether they can successfully avert more deadly conflict.

Domestic / international

References

Acemoglu, Daron, David Autor, David Dorn, Gordon H. Hanson, and Brendan Price. 2016. "Import Competition and the Great U.S. Employment Sag of the 2000s." *Journal of Labor Economics*. Vol. 34, No. S1, S141–98.

AFL-CIO. 2010. "Statement by AFL-CIO President Richard Trumka on the Obama Administration Acceptance of 301 Trade Case." *Inside US Trade*. October 15, 2010.

AIIB. 2020. *2019 AIIB Annual Report and Financials*. AIIB. https://bit.ly /3nBMKn8.

Allison, Graham T. 2017. *Destined for War: Can America and China Escape Thucydides's Trap?* Boston, MA: Houghton Mifflin Harcourt.

Allison, Graham T. and Gregory F. Treverton eds. 1992. *Rethinking America's Security: Beyond Cold War to New World Order*. New York: W. W. Norton.

AmCham China. 2013, 2014, 2015, 2016, 2017, 2018, and 2019. *China Business Climate Survey Report*. Beijing: Amcham China.

Anderson, Perry. 2011. "Lula's Brazil." *London Review of Books*, March 31.

Appelbaum, Richard, Cong Cao, Xueying Han, Rachel Parker, and Denis Simon. 2018. *Innovation in China: Challenging the Global Science and Technology System*. Oxford: Polity.

Arrighi, Giovanni. 1994. *The Long Twentieth Century: Money, Power, and the Origins of Our Times*. New York and London: Verso.

Arrighi, Giovanni. 2007. *Adam Smith in Beijing: Lineages of the 21st Century*. New York and London: Verso.

Arrighi, Giovanni and Beverly Silver. 1999. *Chaos and Governance in the Modern World-System*. Minneapolis: University of Minnesota Press.

Autor, David H., David Dorn, and Gordon H. Hanson. 2016. "The China Shock: Learning from Labor-Market Adjustment to Large Changes in Trade." *Annual Review of Economics*. Vol. 8, 205–40.

Balding, Christopher. 2017. "Venezuela's Road to Disaster Is Littered with Chinese Cash." *Foreign Policy*, June 6.

Barnathan, Joyce. 1994. "China's Gates Swing Open." *Bloomberg*, June 13.

Bergsten, C. Fred. 2005. *The United States and the World Economy: Foreign Economic Policy for the Next Decade*. New York: Columbia University Press.

Bernstein, Richard and Ross H. Monro. 1997. *The Coming Conflict with China*. New York: Knopf.

Bersch, Julia and Graciela L. Kaminsky. 2008. "Financial Globalization in the 19th Century: Germany as a Financial Center." Working paper, George Washington University. https://bit.ly/3FB57yR.

Bienefeld, Manfred. 2000. "Structural Adjustment: Debt Collection Device or Development Policy?" *Review: Fernand Braudel Center*. Vol. 23, No. 4, 533–82.

Blanchette, Jude. 2021. "Beijing's Visions of American Decline." *Politico*, March 11.

Blumenthal, Dan. 2020. "China's Steps Backward Began under Hu Jintao: Beijing's New Aggression and Ideological Reaction Started Well Before Xi Jinping." *Foreign Policy*, June 4.

Blustein, Paul. 2019. *Schism: China, America, and the Fracturing of the Global Trading System*. Waterloo, Ontario: CIGI Press.

Bolande, H. Asher. 2001. "AT&T's Years of Lobbying in China Yield a Minority Stake in Web Venture." *Wall Street Journal*, June 27. www.wsj.com/articles/SB993598166865781749.

Bower, Ernest Z. 2010. "China's Activities in Southeast Asia and Implications for U.S. Interests. Statement Before the US–China Economic and Security Review Commission, February 4, 2010." https://bit.ly/30Kmga2.

Brautigam, Deborah. 2011. *The Dragon's Gift: The Real Story of China in Africa*. New York: Oxford University Press.

Brautigam, Deborah. 2020. "A Critical Look at Chinese 'Debt-Trap Diplomacy': The Rise of a Meme." *Area Development and Policy*. Vol. 5, No. 1, 1–14.

Brenner, Robert. 2003. *The Boom and the Bubble: The US and the World Economy*. London: Verso.

Callahan, William 2005. "How to Understand China: The Dangers and Opportunities of Being a Rising Power." *Review of International Studies*. Vol. 31, No. 4 (October 2005), 701–14.

Campbell, Kurt and Ely Ratner. 2018. "The China Reckoning: How Beijing Defied American Expectations." *Foreign Affairs*. Vol. 92, No. 2, 60–70.

Campbell, Steven. 2015. "China's Human Rights and US–China Economic Relations: Interest Group Lobbying and China's MFN Trade Status." *The International Journal of Social Sciences*. Vol. 33, No. 1, 1–17.

Caixin. n.d. Manufacturing PMI Index. www.caixinglobal.com/report/.

Chang, Che. 2020. "The Nazi Inspiring China's Communists: A decades-Old Legal Argument Used by Hitler Has Found Support in Beijing." *The Atlantic*, December 1.

Chen, Lulu Yilun. 2018. "China Claims More Patents Than Any Country – Most Are Worthless." *Bloomberg*, September 27. https://bit.ly/3HGUX1y.

China Daily. 2021. "Sany 2020 Excavator Sales Top World for First Time," June 3.

China–Latin America Cross-Council Taskforce. 2013. "Chinese Foreign Direct Investment in Latin America and the Caribbean." Economic Commission for Latin America and the Caribbean, United Nations. https://bit.ly/3x8rpou.

Choi, Eun, John Wagner Givens, Andrew W. MacDonald. 2021. "From Power Balancing to Dominant Faction in Xi Jinping's China" China Quarterly, 1–22. https://doi.org/10.1017/S0305741021000473.

Colby, Elbridge A. and A. Wess Mitchell. 2020. "The Age of Great-Power Competition: How the Trump Administration Refashioned American Strategy." Foreign Affairs. Vol. 99, No. 1, 118–30.

Congressional Research Service. 2019. "BUILD Act: Frequently Asked Questions about the New U.S. International Development Finance Corporation." https://fas.org/sgp/crs/misc/R45461.pdf.

Dalton, Matthew and Diana Kinch. 2011. "Debate on Yuan Manipulation Moves to WTO." Wall Street Journal, November 16.

Davis, Bob and Lingling Wei. 2020a. Superpower Showdown: How the Battle between Trump and Xi Threatens a New Cold War. New York: Harper Business.

Davis, Bob and Lingling Wei. 2020b. "The Soured Romance between China and Corporate America." Wall Street Journal, June 5.

De Graaf, Nana, Tobias ten Brink, and Inderjeet Parmar. 2020. "China's Rise in a Liberal World Order in Transition" Review of International Political Economy. Vol. 27, No. 2, 191–207.

Defever, Fabrice and Alejandro Riaño. 2013. "China's Pure Exporter Subsidies: Protectionism by Exporting." VOXEU, January 4. https://bit.ly/3nEiOXS.

Department of Justice. 2018. "Court Imposes Maximum Fine on Sinovel Wind Group for Theft of Trade Secrets." Office of Public Affairs, July 6. https://bit.ly/30NdCYU.

Destler, Irving M. 2005. American Trade Politics. New York: Peterson Institute for International Economics.

Dolan, Chris J. and Jerel A. Rosati. 2006. "U.S. Foreign Economic Policy and the Significance of the National Economic Council." International Studies Perspectives. Vol. 7, No. 2, 102–23.

Dongxing Securities. 2019. Wajueji shendu baogao [Deep Report on Excavating Machines]. August 19. http://pdf.dfcfw.com/pdf/H3_AP2019 08211344797878_1.pdf.

Dreiling, Michael C. and Derek Y. Darves. 2016. *Agents of Neoliberal Globalization: Corporate Networks, State Structures, and Trade Policy.* New York: Cambridge University Press.

Duhigg, Charles and Keith Bradsher. 2012. "How the U.S. Lost Out on iPhone Work." *New York Times*, January 21.

Eichengreen, Barry. 2011. *Exorbitant Privilege: The Rise and Fall of the Dollar and the Future of the International Monetary System.* Oxford: Oxford University Press.

ENR. 2014. "Pushback against Chinese Workers Escalates in Africa." *Engineering News Record*, October 14.

Feng, John. 2020. "'No Turning Back' U.S.–China Relations under Biden, Taiwan Security Analyst Says." *Newsweek*, November 10.

Ferguson, Niall. 2019. "The New Cold War? It Is with China, and It Has Already Begun." *New York Times*, December 2.

Ferguson, Niall and Moritz Schularick. 2007. "'Chimerica' and the Global Asset Market Boom." *International Finance*. Vol. 10, No. 3, 215–39.

Fewsmith, Joseph and Andrew Nathan. 2019. "Authoritarian Resilience Revisited: Joseph Fewsmith with Response from Andrew J. Nathan." *Journal of Contemporary China*. Vol. 28, No. 116, 167–79.

Flanigan, James. 1994. "Clinton's Game of Chicken with China." *Los Angeles Times*, March 16. www.latimes.com/archives/la-xpm-1994-03-16-fi-34783-story.html.

Forbes. 2005. "Turning Corn into Clothing." *Forbes*, July 10. www.forbes.com /global/2005/0110/020sidebar.html?sh=33e8c2de6306.

Foreign Affairs. 2020. "Should U.S. Foreign Policy Focus on Great-Power Competition? Foreign Affairs Asks the Experts." *Foreign Affairs*, October 13. https://fam.ag/3cB1Kve.

Foster, Peter. 2010. "WikiLeaks: China's Politburo a Cabal of Business Empires." *The Telegraph*, December 6. https://bit.ly/3qTh5zT.

Frayer, Lauren. 2019. "In Sri Lanka, China's Building Spree Is Raising Questions About Sovereignty." *NPR*, December 13. https://n.pr/3FsOlSs.

French, Howard. 2011. "In Africa, an Election Reveals Skepticism of Chinese Involvement." *The Atlantic*, September 29.

Frontier Services Group. 2017. "Frontier Services Group Strategy Update." Press Release, December 19. https://bit.ly/3qXMXU6.

Fukuyama, Francis. 1992. *The End of History and the Last Man.* New York: Free Press.

Fuller, Douglas. 2016. *Paper Tigers, Hidden Dragons: Firms and the Political Economy of China's Technological Development.* Oxford and New York: Oxford University Press.

Gallagher, Kevin and Roberto Porzecanski. 2010. *The Dragon in the Room: China and the Future of Latin American Industrialization* Stanford, CA: Stanford University Press.

Garvin, Francis J. 2003. "Ideas, Power, and the Politics of America's International Monetary Policy during the 1960s." in Jonathan Krishner, ed., *Monetary Orders: Ambiguous Economics, Ubiquitous Politics*. Ithaca, NY: Cornell University Press, 195–217.

Gelpern, Anna, Sebastian Horn, Scott Morris, Brad Parks, and Christoph Trebesch. 2021. "How China Lends: A Rare Look into 100 Debt Contracts with Foreign Governments." Working Paper, Center for Global Development. https://bit.ly/3DDEcSD.

Gerth, Jeff. 1998. "US Business Role in Policy on China Is Questioned." *New York Times*, April 13. https://nyti.ms/3kV2QGV.

Gerth, Jeff and David Sanger. 1998. "How Chinese Won Rights to Launch Satellites for US." *New York Times*, May 17. https://nyti.ms/32b5xgS.

Gokey, Malarie. 2014. "Obama Defends NSA Spying on Huawei – Furious China Demands Explanation." *Tech Times*, March 24.

Gonzalez, Anabel. 2018. "Latin America–China Trade and Investment amid Global Tension: A Need to Upgrade and Diversify." Atlantic Council's Adrienne Arsht Latin America Center, December.

Guo, Rui and He Huifeng. 2020. "Don't Assume US–China Relations Will Get Better under Joe Biden, Government Adviser Warns." *South China Morning Post*, November 22. https://bit.ly/3HHbYsf.

Haglung, Dan. 2019. "In It for the Long Term? Governance and Learning among Chinese Investors in Zambia's Copper Sector." *The China Quarterly*. Vol. 199, 627–46.

Hamashita, Takeshi. 2008. *China, East Asia, and the World Economy: Regional and Historical Perspectives*. New York: Routledge.

Hameed, Maham. 2018. "Infrastructure and Democracy – A Case of China–Pakistan Economic Corridor." Ho-fung Hung, ed., Special Session on "China and the Global South," *Palgrave Communications* No. 4. https://doi.org/10.1057/s41599-018-0115-7.

Hardt, Michael and Antonio Negri. 2000. *Empire*. Cambridge, MA: Harvard University Press.

Harvey, David. 2005. *The New Imperialism*. Oxford: Oxford University Press.

Harvey, David. 2007. *A Brief History of Neoliberalism*. Oxford: Oxford University Press.

Heritage Foundation. 1979. "Most Favored Nation Status: Trade with Communist Countries." Heritage Foundation Backgrounder No. 83, May 7.

Hillman, Jonathan E. 2018 "China's Belt and Road Initiative: Five Years Later." Center for Strategic and International Studies. https://bit.ly/3FyLJCt.

Hobson, John Atkinson. 2018 [1902]. *Imperialism: A Study of the History, Politics, and Economics of the Colonial Powers in Europe and America.* Adonsonia Press.

Holmes, Stanley. 1996. "Boeing's Campaign to Protect a Market – Corporations Lobby to Save China Trade." *Seattle Times*, May 27.

Homeland Security News Wire. 2007. "White House Plans to Weaken CFIUS Security Review Powers." *Homeland Security News Wire*, November 12.

Hook, Leslie. 2013. "Caterpillar Digs into Trouble in China." *Financial Times*, February 11. www.ft.com/content/5dc97f12-7363-11e2-9e92-001 44feabdc0.

Hopewell, Kristen. 2016. *Breaking the WTO: How Emerging Powers Disrupted the Neoliberal Project.* Stanford, CA: Stanford University Press.

Horn, Sebastian, Carmen M. Reinhart, and Christoph Trebesch. 2019. "China's Overseas Lending." IMF ARC, November 7. https://bit.ly/3oKGrgI.

Hu, Albert G. Z., Peng Zhang, and Lijing Zhao. 2017. "China as Number One? Evidence from China's Most Recent Patenting Surge." *Journal of Developing Economics*. Vol. 124, 107–19.

Hung, Ho-fung. 2015. "China Steps Back." *New York Times*, April 6.

Hung, Ho-fung. 2016. *The China Boom: Why China Will Not Rule the World.* New York: Columbia University Press.

Hung, Ho-fung. 2018. "Global Capitalism in the Age of Trump." *Contexts*. Vol. 17, No. 3, 40–45.

Hung, Ho-fung. 2020a. "The Periphery in the Making of Globalization: The China Lobby and the Reversal of Clinton's China Trade Policy, 1993–1994." *Review of International Political Economy*. Vol. 28, No. 4, 1004–27.

Hung, Ho-fung. 2020b. "How Capitalist Is China?" *Socio-Economic Review.* Vol. 18, No. 3, 888–92.

Hung, Ho-fung. 2020c. "China and the Global South." In Thomas Fingar and Jean Oi, eds., *Fateful Decisions: Choices That Will Shape China's Future.* Palo Alto, CA: Stanford University Press, 247–71.

Hung, Ho-fung. In press. *City on the Edge: Hong Kong under Chinese Rule.* New York and Cambridge: Cambridge University Press.

Hung, Ho-fung and Daniel Thompson. 2016. "Money Supply, Class Power, and Inflation: Monetarism Reassessed." *American Sociological Review.* Vol. 81, No. 3, 447–66.

Huntington, Samuel. 1996. *The Clash of Civilizations and the Remaking of World Order.* New York: Simon and Shuster.

Ikenberry, G. John. 2004. "Illusions of Empire: Defining the New American Order." *Foreign Affairs*, March/April.

Inside US Trade. 1994a. "State Protests Rubin Comments on Easing Conditions for China MFN," February 4. https://bit.ly/3DzA4mq.

Inside US Trade. 1994b. "Pelosi Blasts Proposals for Lifting Conditions on China MFN," February 11. https://bit.ly/3kVOEO1.

Inside US Trade. 2010. "Fair Currency Coalition Sends Petition to Ryan, Murphy Urging Currency Legislation," September 15. https://bit.ly /3HAxYFr.

Inside US Trade. 2011. "FTA Supporters Say U.S. Firms Losing out to China in Colombian Market," February 22. https://bit.ly/3CEgbJM.

Inside US Trade. 2012. "'Special 301' IPR Report Makes Few Changes to Country Designations," May 4. https://bit.ly/3CCI1Ge.

Inside US Trade. 2015a. "USCBC Statement on Introduced Congressional Currency Legislation," February 10. https://bit.ly/3Fys3if.

Inside US Trade. 2015b. "Backers of CVD Currency Bill Rejected IMF Assessment That Yuan Is Not Undervalued," May 29. https://bit.ly /3CCu9Mb.

Inside US Trade. 2015c. "China Currency Critics Blast New Devaluation, But Others See Market Shift," August 11. https://bit.ly/3FAkPKF.

Inside US Trade. 2017. "Survey: U.S. Businesses in China Hold Growing IP, Competition Concerns," December 7. https://bit.ly/3kRJhPG.

Institute of International Finance. 2020. "Global Debt Monitor: Sharp Spike in Debt Ratios." Institute of International Finance, July 16. https://bit.ly /3HFeU8U.

International Trade Administration (US Department of Commerce), 2020. "Steel Export Report: China," May 2020. https://legacy.trade.gov/steel/coun tries/pdfs/exports-china.pdf.

Jepson, Nicholas. 2020. *In China's Wake: How the Commodity Boom Transformed Development Strategies in the Global South*. New York: Columbia University Press.

JHU CARI. n.d. China in Africa Research Initiative Database. www.sais-cari.org/data.

Jiang, Shigong. 2019. "The Internal Logic of Super-Sized Political Entities: 'Empire' and World Order" (translated by David Ownby). *Reading the China Dream*. www.readingthechinadream.com/jiang-shigong-empire-and-world-order.html.

Johnson, Geoff. 2000. "AT&T's China Foray Is Promising Development for Telecommunications Carriers." Gartner Research. .

Jones, Bruce. 2020. "China and the Return of Great Power Strategic Competition." Brookings Institution.

Kahn, Imran. 2020. "IMF Asks Pakistan to Reduce 'Trade and Commerce Reliance' on China." *Business Standard*, February 14. https://bit.ly /3DGMhWt.

Kang, David C. 2010. *East Asia before the West: Five Centuries of Trade and Tribute*. New York: Columbia University Press.

Kaplan, Robert. 2019. "A New Cold War Has Begun." *Foreign Policy*, January 7. https://foreignpolicy.com/2019/01/07/a-new-cold-war-has-begun /.

Karl, Terry Lynn. 1997 *The Paradox of Plenty: Oil Booms and Petro-States*. Berkeley, CA: University of California Press.

Kauko, Karlo. 2020. "The Vanishing Interest Income of Chinese Banks as an Indicator of Loan Quality Problems." VOX EU CEPR, May 22.

Kautsky, Karl. 1914. "Ultraimperialism." *Die Neue Zeit*, September 11.

Kazeem, Yomi. 2020. "The Truth about Africa's 'debt problem' with China." *Quartz*, October 8. https://qz.com/africa/1915076/how-bad-is-africas-debt-to-china/.

Kelemen, Barbara. 2019. "China's Changing Response to Militancy in Pakistan." International Institute for Strategic Studies, September 2. www .iiss.org/blogs/analysis/2019/09/csdp-militancy-in-pakistan.

Kennedy, Paul. 1980. *The Rise of the Anglo–German Antagonism, 1860–1914*. London: George Allen & Unwin.

Kennedy, Scott. 2020. "The Biggest But Not the Strongest: China's Place in the Fortune Global 500." CSIS Report, August 18. https://bit.ly/3cBdVZg.

KHL. 2021. Yellow Table 2021. https://bit.ly/3FDEtWi.

King, Neil. 2005. "Inside Pentagon, a Scholar Shapes Views of China." *Wall Street Journal*, Sept 8.

Kirchgaessner, Stephanie. 2010. "Former US Official Joins Huawei Consultancy." *Financial Times*, October 20.

Klein, Matthew C. and Michael Pettis. 2020. *Trade Wars Are Class Wars: How Rising Inequality Distorts the Global Economy and Threatens International Peace*. Princeton, NJ: Princeton University Press.

Koons, Cynthia. 2013. "Skepticism on China's Nonperforming Loans Despite Strong Data, Values of Country's Leading Banks Decline in Reflection of Investor Worries About Credit Quality." *Wall Street Journal*, December 3.

Kranish, Michael. 2018. "Trumps China Whisperer: How Billionaire Stephen Schwarzman Has Sought to Keep the President Close to Beijing." *Washington Post*, March 11. https://wapo.st/3pHAVNN.

Krasner, Stephen D. 1978. *Defending the National Interest: Raw Materials Investments and U.S. Foreign Policy.* Princeton, NJ: Princeton University Press.

Krause, Lawrence B. 1998. "The Economics and Politics of the Asian Financial Crisis of 1997–98." New York: Council on Foreign Relations.

Krueger, Alan B. 2000. "Economic Scene; Honest Brokers Separate Policy from Sausage for the White House." *New York Times*, November 9.

Kuo, L. Jay. 1994. "Farewell to Jackson-Vanik: The Case for Unconditional MFN Status for the People's Republic of China." *Asian American Law Journal.* Vol. 1, No. 85, 85–116.

Lampton, David M. 1994. "America's China Policy in the Age of the Finance Minister: Clinton Ends Linkage." *China Quarterly.* No. 139, 597–621.

Lardy, Nicholas. 2019. *The State Strikes Back: The End of Economic Reform in China?* Washington, DC: Peterson Institute for International Economics.

Lau, Justine. 2006. "AT&T Executive Calls for China Deregulation." *Financial Times*, April 6.

Leary, Alex and Bob Davis. 2021. "Biden's China Policy Is Emerging – and It Looks a Lot Like Trump's." *Wall Street Journal*, June 10.

Lee, Ching Kwan. 2017. *The Specter of Global China: Politics, Labor, and Foreign Investment in Africa.* Chicago, IL: University of Chicago Press.

LEM. 2006. "Beleaguered: Apple Bottoms Out, 1996 to 1998." *Low End Mac*, September 29. http://lowendmac.com/2006/beleaguered-apple-bottoms-out -1996-to-1998/.

Lenin, Vladimir Ilyich. 1963 [1917]. "Imperialism, the Highest Stage of Capitalism." In *Lenin: Selected Works, Volume 1.* Moscow: Progress Publishers, 1963, 667–766.

Lew, Jacob J., Gary Roughead, Jennifer Hillman, and David Sacks. 2021. "China's Belt and Road: Implications for the United States." New York: Council on Foreign Relations.

Lexis/Nexis. n.d. Lexis Uni Database. https://bit.ly/3CzTm9X.

Lieberthal, Kenneth. 2011. "The American Pivot to Asia." Brookings Institution, December 21. www.brookings.edu/articles/the-american-pivot- to-asia/.

Liu, Mingxiang, Victor Shih, and Dong Zhang. 2018. "The Fall of the Old Guards: Explaining Decentralization in China." *Studies in Comparative and International Development.* Vol. 53, 379–403.

Lombardi, Domenico and Anton Malkin. 2017. "Domestic Politics and External Financial Liberalization in China: The Capacity and Fragility of External Market Pressure." *Journal of Contemporary China.* Vol. 26, No. 108, 785–800. https://doi.org/10.1080/10670564.2017.1337291.

Luo, Yadong. 2000. *How to Enter China: Choices and Lessons*. Ann Arbor, MI: University of Michigan Press.

Lyons, Paul. 2021. *Winning without Warring? The Geostrategic Implications of China's Foreign Direct Investments on Southeast Asia and the South China Sea Sovereignty Disputes*. Doctor of International Affairs Dissertation, School of Advanced International Studies, Johns Hopkins University.

Macfarlane, Laurie. 2020. "A Spectre Is Haunting the West – the Spectre of Authoritarian Capitalism." *Open Democracy*, April 16. https://bit.ly /3CCHVhG.

Mandhana, Niharika, Warren P. Strobel, and Feliz Solomon. 2021. "Coup Puts Myanmar at the Center of U.S.–China Clash." *Wall Street Journal*, February 2.

Maranto, Lauren. 2020. "Who Benefits from China's Cybersecurity Laws?" Center for Strategic and International Studies, June 25. https://bit.ly /316WgpT.

Marino, Rich. 2018. *Chinese Trade: Trade Deficits, State Subsidies and the Rise of China*. London and New York: Routledge.

Matsumoto, Norio and Naoki Watanabe. 2020. "Huawei's Base Station Teardown Shows Dependence on US-Made Parts." *Nikkei Asia*, October 12. https://s.nikkei.com/3Cidka3.

McMeekin, Sean. 2012. *The Berlin–Baghdad Express: The Ottoman Empire and Germany's Bid for World Power*. Cambridge, MA: Harvard University Press.

Menn, Joseph. 2012. "White House-Ordered Review Found No Evidence of Huawei Spying: Sources." *Reuters*, October 17.

Meredith, Robyn. 2010. "Growing Bearish." *Forbes*. February 10. https://bit.ly /3GnXxZB.

Merics. 2019. "China's Caution about Loosening Cross-Border Capital Flows." Merics, June 19. https://merics.org/en/report/chinas-caution-about-loosening -cross-border-capital-flows.

Meyers, Steven Lee. 2020. "Buffeted by Trump, China Has Little Hope for Warmer Relations with Biden." *New York Times*, November 9. www .nytimes.com/2020/11/09/world/asia/china-united-states-biden.html.

Milanovic, Branko. 2019. "With the US and China, Two Types of Capitalism Are Competing with Each Other." *Promarket*, September 25. https://bit.ly /3DIuHS0.

Miller, Maggie. 2019. "Trump Reversal on Huawei Gets Bipartisan Pushback." *The Hill*, July 2. https://bit.ly/3oTZwx4.

Milward, Alan S. (1985) "The Reichsmark Bloc and the International Economy." In H. W. Koch, ed., *Aspects of the Third Reich*. London: Palgrave, 331–59.

Mining. 2020. "Liebherr Mining Settles Lawsuit over Copycat Allegations." *Mining,* August 10. https://bit.ly/3x5joRq.

Ministry of Commerce, People's Republic of China. 2010. *Statistical Bulletin of China's Outward Foreign Direct Investment.*

Ministry of Commerce, People's Republic of China, 2015. *Statistical Bulletin of China's Outward Foreign Direct Investment.*

Ministry of Commerce, People's Republic of China. 2019. *Statistical Bulletin of China's Outward Foreign Direct Investment.*

Mintz, John. 1998. "Missile Failures Led to Loral–China Link." *Washington Post*, June 12. https://wapo.st/3cAuynS.

National Bureau of Statistics of China. n.d. *China Statistical Yearbook* (various years). www.stats.gov.cn/english/Statisticaldata/AnnualData/.

Niewenhuis, Lucas. 2020. "China's Belt and Road Lending Dries up." *SupChina*, December 8. https://bit.ly/3kWOd5Y.

Nouwens, Meia. 2018. "Guardians of the Belt and Road." International Institute for Strategic Studies. www.iiss.org/blogs/research-paper/2018/08/guardians-belt-and-road.

NYA International. 2015, "Kidnapping Risk to Chinese Nationals." Global Kidnap for Ransom Update, April. https://bit.ly/3kVQIFL.

Nye, Joseph. 1991. *Bound To Lead: The Changing Nature Of American Power.* New York: Basic Books.

O'Connor, James. 2011. "State Building, Infrastructure Development and Chinese Energy Projects in Myanmar." Irasec's Discussion Papers, No. 10. www.irasec.com/documents/fichiers/46.pdf.

Pae, Peter. 2003. "Boeing, Hughes to Pay $32 Million for Helping China with Technology." *Los Angeles Times*, March 6. https://lat.ms/3nu7egt.

Panitch, Leo and Sam Gindin. 2013. *The Making Of Global Capitalism: The Political Economy Of American Empire.* London and New York: Verso.

Parameswaran, Prashanth. 2019. "Malaysia's Evolving Approach to China's Belt and Road Initiative." *The Diplomat*, April 23. https://bit.ly/3nAHtw5.

Pearson, Margaret, Meg Rithmire, and Kellee Tsai. 2020. "Party–State Capitalism in China." Harvard Business School Working Paper. https://hbswk.hbs.edu/item/party-state-capitalism-in-china.

Pham, Sherissa. 2019. "Losing Huawei as a Customer Could Cost US Tech Companies $11 Billion." *CNN*, May 17. www.cnn.com/2019/05/17/tech/huawei-us-ban-suppliers/index.html.

Pillsbury, Michael. 2015. *The Hundred-Year Marathon: China's Secret Strategy to Replace America as the Global Superpower.* New York: Henry Holt & Company.

Posen, Adam S. 2008. "Why the Euro Will Not Rival the Dollar." *International Finance*. Vol. 11, No. 1, 75–100.

Prasad, Monica. 2012. *The Land of Too Much: American Abundance and the Paradox of Poverty*. Cambridge, MA: Harvard University Press.

Prince, Marcelo and Willa Plank. 2012. "A Short History of Apple's Manufacturing in the U.S." *Wall Street Journal*, December 6.

Qi, Zheng. 2012. "Carl Schmitt in China." *Telos*. Vol. 2012, No. 160 (Fall), 29–52.

Radio Free Asia. 2019. "Mahathir: Malaysia Saves Billions in Renegotiated Railway Deal with China." *Radio Free Asia*, April 15. www.rfa.org/english/news/china/malaysia-railway-04152019170804.html.

Reuters. 2011. "Remarks by Obama and Hu at Washington News Conference." *Reuters*, January 19. https://reut.rs/3nMhktt.

Reuters. 2019. "Erik Prince Company to Build Training Centre in China's Xinjiang," *Reuters*, January 31. https://reut.rs/3ntBFUb.

Roache, Shaun K. 2012. "China's Impact on World Commodity Market." IMF Working Paper.

Robinson, William. 1996. *Promoting Polyarchy: Globalization, US Intervention, and Hegemony*. New York: Cambridge University Press.

Roy, Danny. 2019. "Assertive China: Irredentism or Expansionism?" *Survival: Global Politics and Strategy*. Vol. 61, No. 1, 51–74.

Runde, Daniel and Richard Olson. 2018. "An Economic Crisis in Pakistan Again: What's Different This Time?" Center for Strategic and International Studies, October 31. https://bit.ly/3HGpqwH.

Rutkowski, Ryan. 2015. "Deleveraging the State in China." Peterson Institute of International Economics, January 26. www.piie.com/blogs/china-economic-watch/deleveraging-state-china.

Sala, Ilaria Maria. 2017. "More Neighbors Are Saying 'No Thanks' to Chinese Money – For Now." *Quartz*, December 4.

Sanusi, Lamido. 2013. "Africa Must Get Real about Chinese Ties." *Financial Times*, March 11.

SANY. n.d. "One Belt, One Road: SANY's New Engine for Business Globalization." https://trends.directindustry.com/sany/project-52887-157428.html.

Schmidt, Michael S., Keith Bradsher, and Christine Hauser. 2012. "U.S. Panel Cites Risks in Chinese Equipment." *New York Times*, October 8.

Schoenberger, Karl. 1994. "Human Rights in China or Jobs in California? Clinton's MFN Decision Poses a Question of Conscience." *Los Angeles Times*, May 15. www.latimes.com/archives/la-xpm-1994-05-15-fi-57984-story.html.

Scott, Robert E. and Zane Mokhiber. 2018. "The China Toll Deepens: Growth in the Bilateral Trade Deficit between 2001 and 2017 Cost 3.4 Million U.S. Jobs, with Losses in Every State and Congressional District." Economic Policy Institute Report, October 23. https://bit.ly/3be6RAS.

Sebenius, James and Ellen Knebel. 2010. "Bill Nichol Negotiates with Walmart: Hard Bargains over Soft Goods." Harvard Business School Case Study, 9-910-043.

Secretary of Senate. n.d. Lobbying Disclosure Act Reports Database. https://lda .senate.gov/system/public/.

Shafer, D. Michael. 1994. *Winners and Losers: How Sectors Shape the Developmental Prospects of States*. Ithaca, NY: Cornell University Press.

Shah, Saeed and Uditha Jayasinghe. 2020. "China Regains Clout in Sri Lanka with Family's Return to Power." *Wall Street Journal*, November 28. https:// on.wsj.com/3xm9g77.

Shirk, Susan. 2018 "China in Xi's 'New Era': The Return to Personalistic Rule." *Journal of Democracy*. Vol. 29, No. 2, 22–36.

Silver, Beverly. 2003. *Forces of Labor: Workers' Movement and Globalization since 1870*. New York: Cambridge University Press.

Silverstein, Ken. 2007. "The New China Hands." *The Nation*, October 23.

Skocpol, Theda. 1985. "Bringing the State Back In: Strategies of Analysis in Current Research." In Peter Evans, Dietrich Rueschemeyer, and Theda Skocpol, eds., *Bringing the State Back In*. Cambridge: Cambridge University Press, 3–38.

Skonieczny, Amy. 2018. "Trading with the Enemy: Narrative, Identity and US Trade Politics." *Review of International Political Economy*. Vol. 25, No. 4, 441–62.

Sly, Maria Jose Haro. 2017. "The Argentine Portion of the Soybean Commodity Chain." *Palgrave Communications*. Vol. 4. https://doi.org/10.1057/pal comms.2017.95.

Smith, Hedrick. 2012. *Who Stole the American Dream?* New York: Random House.

Stein, Judith. 2011. *Pivotal Decade: How the United States Traded Factories for Finance in the Seventies*. New Haven, CT: Yale University Press.

Stiglitz, Joseph. 2002. *Globalization and Its Discontents*. New York: W. W. Norton and Company.

Storey, Ian and Herbert Yee. eds. 2002. *The China Threat: Perceptions, Myths and Reality*. London and New York: Routledge.

Strange, Susan. 1980. "Germany and the World Monetary System." In Wilfrid Kohl and Giorgio Basevi, eds., *West Germany: A European and Global Power*. Lexington, KY: Lexington Books, 45–62.

Strangio, Sebastian. 2020. "In UN Speech, Duterte Stiffens Philippines' Stance on the South China Sea." *The Diplomat*, September 23. https://bit.ly/3Ejsex8.

Strohecker, Karin. 2019. "REFILE-China-Backed AIIB Eyes More 2019 Bond Sales After Dollar Debut." *Reuters*, May 9. https://reut.rs/3mfso2H.

Sutter, Robert G. 1998. *U.S. Policy Toward China: An Introduction to the Role of Interest Groups*. Lantham, MD: Rowman & Littlefield.

US Chamber of Commerce and American Chamber of Commerce China. 2017. *A Blueprint for Action: Addressing Priority Issues of Concern in U.S.–China Commercial Relations*. Washington, DC: US Chamber of Commerce and American Chamber of Commerce China.

US–China Business Council. 2014. "Competition Policy and Enforcement in China." https://bit.ly/3cyq5lp.

US–China Economic and Security Review Commission. 2019. "2019 Report to Congress." https://bit.ly/3qTsqQo.

US Congress. 1993. Congressional Record, Senate, June 8. www.congress.gov/103/crecb/1993/06/08/GPO-CRECB-1993-pt9-3-2.pdf.

US Congress. 1994a. Congressional Record, House of Representatives, March 21. www.congress.gov/103/crecb/1994/03/21/GPO-CRECB-1994-pt4-7-2.pdf.

US Congress. 1994b. Congressional Record, House of Representatives, August 9. https://bit.ly/3nDoDoe.

Van Apeldoorn, Bastiaan and Naná de Graaff. 2016. *American Grand Strategy and Corporate Elite Networks: The Open Door since the End of the Cold War*. New York: Routledge

Vyas, Kejal and Anatoly Kurmanaev. 2017. "Goldman Sachs Bought Venezuela's State Oil Company's Bonds Last Week." *Wall Street Journal*, May 28.

Wagreich, Samuel. 2013. "Lobbying by Proxy: A Study of China's Lobbying Practices in the United States, 1979–2010 and the Implications for FARA." *Journal of Politics and Society*. Vol. 24, No. 1, 130–60.

Walt, Stephen M. 2018. *The Hell of Good Intentions: America's Foreign Policy Elite and the Decline of U.S. Primacy*. New York: Farrar, Straus and Giroux.

Walter, Carl E. and Fraser J. T. Howie. 2012. *Red Capitalism: The Fragile Financial Foundation of China's Extraordinary Rise*. Singapore: John Wiley & Sons.

Wang, Celine 2017, "China and Zambia's Resource Nationalism." *East Asia Forum*, March 31. https://bit.ly/3HSdJmT.

Wang, Yingyao. 2015. "The Rise of the 'Shareholding State': Financialization of Economic Management in China." *Socio-Economic Review*. Vol. 13, No. 3, 603–25.

Warwick, William. 1994. "A Review of AT&T's Business History in China: The Memorandum of Understanding in Context." *Telecommunications Policy.* Vol. 18, No. 3, 265–74.

Washington Post. 1998. "Chinese Missile Allegations: Key Stories." https://wapo.st/3oQsrlh.

Weber, Max. 2013 [1922]. *Economy and Society: Volume I.* Berkeley and Los Angeles, CA: University of California Press.

Wei, Lingling and Bob Davis. 2018. "How China Systematically Pries Technology from U.S. Companies: Beijing Leans on an Array of Levers to Extract Intellectual Property – Sometimes Coercively." *Wall Street Journal*, September 26. https://on.wsj.com/3x73ar1.

Weinberger, Matt. 2017. "The Story of How Steve Jobs Saved Apple from Disaster and Led It to Rule the World." *Business Insider*, January 1.

Weisskopf, Michael. 1993. "Backbone of the New China Lobby: U.S. Firms." *Washington Post*, June 14. https://wapo.st/3FrLYPU.

Wernau, Julie. 2018. "Venezuela Is in Default, but Goldman Sachs Just Got Paid." *Wall Street Journal*, April 10. https://on.wsj.com/3x62amZ.

WIPO. 2020. "China Becomes Top Filer of International Patents in 2019 amid Robust Growth for WIPO's IP Services, Treaties and Finances." World Intellectual Property Organization, April 7. www.wipo.int/pressroom/en/articles/2020/article_0005.html.

Witkin, Richard. 1972. "US Grants Boeing License to Sell 10 707's to China." *New York Times*, July 6.

World Bank. a n.d. World Development Indicators Databank. https://databank.worldbank.org/source/world-development-indicators.

World Bank b. n.d. International Debt Statistics Databank. https://databank.worldbank.org/source/international-debt-statistics.

Wu, Wendy. 2016. "AIIB and World Bank Reach Deal on Joint Projects, As China-Led Lender Prepares to Approve U. S. $1.2 Billion of Funds This Year." *South China Morning Post*, April 14.

XGMC. 2019. Xugong jituan gongcheng jixie gufen youxian gongshi 2018 niandu baogao [2018 Annual Report of XGMC], April 26. https://bit.ly/3cvAwX7.

Yan, Xu and Douglas Pitt. 2002. *Chinese Telecommunication Policy.* Boston, MA: Artech House.

Yang Jie and Laurie Burkitt. 2014. "China Denies Using Antimonopoly Law to Target Foreign Companies: Unfair Targeting Could Be in Violation of WTO Commitments." *Wall Street Journal*, September 11. https://on.wsj.com/3HGmL6k.

Young, George F. W. 1992. "German Banking and German Imperialism in Latin America in the Wilhelmine Era." *Ibero-amerikanisches Archiv Neue Folge*. Vol. 18, No. 1/2, 31–66.

Yousufzai, Gul. 2020. "Alleged Leader of Chinese Consulate Attack in Pakistan Reported Killed." *Reuters*, December 26. www.reuters.com/article/instant-article/idUSKCN1OP12H.

Zarroli, Jim. 2018. "It Was a Company with a Lot of Promise. Then a Chinese Customer Stole Its Technology." *NPR*, April 9. https://prod-text.npr.org /599557634.

Zeng, Ka. 2004. *Trade Threats, Trade Wars: Bargaining, Retaliation, and American Coercive Diplomacy*. Ann Arbor, MI: University of Michigan Press.

Zenglein, Max J. and Anna Holzmann. 2019. "Evolving Made in China 2025: China's Industrial Policy in the Quest for Global Tech Leadership." Mercator Institute for China Studies. https://bit.ly/3GyJalx.

Zheng, Shuwen. 2019. "Private Security Companies in Kenya and the Impact of Chinese Actors." JHU SAIS Working Paper.

Zhongguo qingnian bao. 2006. "Daguo jueqi: zhongyang zhengzhiju yici jiti xuexide xinwen" [Great Power Rising: News on a Collective Study of the Politburo]. *zhongguo qingnian bao*, November 28.

Zhu Rongji. 2011. *Zhu Rongji Jianghua Shilu* [A Veritable Record of Speeches of Zhu Rongji], Vol. 1. Beijing: Renmin chubanshe.

Zoellick, Robert B. and Justin Yifu Lin. 2009. "Recovery: A Job for China and the U.S." *Washington Post*, March 6.

Global China

Ching Kwan Lee

Hong Kong University of Science and Technology,
University of California-Los Angeles

Ching Kwan Lee is Dr. Chung Sze-yuen Professor of Social Science at the Hong Kong University of Science and Technology and a professor of sociology at the University of California-Los Angeles. Her scholarly interests include political sociology, popular protests, labor, development, political economy, comparative ethnography, China, Hong Kong, East Asia and the Global South. She is the author of three multiple award-winning monographs on contemporary China: *Gender and the South China Miracle: Two Worlds of Factory Women* (1998), *Against the Law: Labor Protests in China's Rustbelt and Sunbelt* (2007) and *The Specter of Global China: Politics, Labor and Foreign Investment in Africa* (2017). Her co-edited volumes include *Take Back Our Future: An Eventful Sociology of Hong Kong's Umbrella Movement* (2019) and *The Social Question in the 21st Century: A Global View* (2019).

About the Series

The Cambridge Elements series Global China showcases thematic, region- or country-specific studies on China's multifaceted global engagements and impacts. Each title, written by a leading scholar of the subject matter at hand, combines a succinct, comprehensive and up-to-date overview of the debates in the scholarly literature with original analysis and a clear argument. Featuring cutting edge scholarship on arguably one of the most important and controversial developments in the 21st century, the Global China Elements series will advance a new direction of China scholarship that expands China Studies beyond China's territorial boundaries.

Cambridge Elements ☰

Global China

Elements in the series

Made in the USA
Las Vegas, NV
28 November 2022